Praise for the first edition of *Business Writing: What Works, What Won't*

"Wilma Davidson gently guides you past the terror of the blank page with humor and practical advice on how to write well. Be sure to include this book in your tool kit for success in business."
—Jon Kraushar, president of Kraushar Communications, debate coach for Dick Cheney, and coauthor with Roger Ailes of *You Are the Message*

"I found your book to be a helpful refresher for me, easy reading, and a valuable tool for those who will never be able to attend one of your seminars. The most pleasant surprise was how effectively you brought the humor of your seminars to the book."
—Stephen J. Burrows, president and CEO of Anheuser-Busch International

"A how-to manual that is invaluable for marketing professionals and the people who manage them."
—Ellen Donahoe-Dalton, president of Dalton Associates Marketing Consultants

"Our members who took Wilma Davidson's course loved her—and *Business Writing: What Works, What Won't*. Without exception, they found the material and its presentation to be excellent."
—Brown University Learning Community

Business Writing
What Works, What Won't
Revised Edition

Wilma Davidson, Ed.D.

St. Martin's Griffin
New York

BUSINESS WRITING: WHAT WORKS, WHAT WON'T: REVISED EDITION. Copyright ©
2001, 1994 by Wilma Davidson, Ed.D. Illustrations copyright © 1994 by Durell
Godfrey. All rights reserved. Most of the illustrations in this book are based on
sketches drawn by Tom Kish and copyright © Davidson & Associates. Printed
in the United States of America. No part of this book may be used or repro-
duced in any manner whatsoever without written permission except in the
case of brief quotations embodied in critical articles or reviews. For information, address St. Martin's Press, 175 Fifth Avenue, New York, N.Y. 10010.

www.stmartins.com

Excerpts taken from *The Winter's Art* column by James J. Kilpatrick. Distrib-
uted by Universal Press Syndicate. Reprinted with permission. All rights
reserved.

Library of Congress Cataloging-in-Publication Data

Davidson, Wilma.
    Business writing: what works, what won't / Wilma Davidson.
        p.   cm.
    ISBN 0-312-10948-2 (pbk)
    1. Business writing.   I. Title.
    HF5718.3.D376   1994
    808'.06665—dc20   94-6056
                                                                        CIP

First Edition: May 2001

10 9 8 7 6 5 4 3 2 1

To my husband, Steve—
and our children, Lisa and Eric

Contents

Foreword

What is it that Wilma Davidson knows? What qualifies her to advise us on what constitutes a winning business memo or monthly report?

As one of the first scholars to earn a doctorate by examining the types of writing unique to business, and as a consultant with twenty years of experience helping corporate employees at all levels hone their business-writing skills, Wilma Davidson knows that most people are afraid of writing. And they're afraid for good reason.

In most schools writing was—and, alas, still is—presented as an assignment attached to an impossible-to-meet deadline. Rarely is advice given on how to navigate between assignment and finished product, advice—simply, centrally, awesomely—on *how to write*. Instead, what unhappily passes for the teaching of writing in too many schools is solely the grading of words on paper, with the reason for that C or D, or even A or B, an inexplicable and never-to-be-explained mystery. Too often students are sent off on a writing assignment—and then on to writing assignments in the corporate world—with no guidelines on *how* to begin or how to know what works and what won't. Fear and anxiety are understandable responses to such a hopeless challenge.

In *Business Writing: What Works, What Won't*, Wilma Davidson demystifies the process of writing, particularly for those of us who must write on the job—and that is almost everyone. She sets forth, using witty and pointed exemplars and exercises, how to overcome writing block; how to "read" what others want you to write; how to meet a range of expectations, from writing a business letter that states its purpose crisply and accurately to composing a report due tomorrow—with all varieties of the writing you must do set out in unpretentious yet carefully edited language, in prose others are compelled to read.

So here is help at last. Avail yourself of some of the best advice on writing you can ever hope to receive. Read. Heed. Practice. Write. Prosper.

—Janet Emig
University Professor Emeritus of English Education
Rutgers, The State University of New Jersey

Acknowledgments

Naturally, many people—some directly, others without realizing it—sparked and subsidized my energies and beliefs during a lifetime of learning. Most especially, however, I thank these individuals, whose uncommon contributions ushered this book into existence.

- My clients and their companies, who, over the years, have responded thoughtfully and enthusiastically to my material and seminars;

- Susan McCloskey, colleague and consultant, who always found order in my seeming disorder and whose gentle and apt suggestions always made sense;

- Ellen Corum, who put my first draft on disk and never complained (well, almost never) about my incessant overhauling of the manuscript's early drafts;

- Janet Emig, who, as my doctoral mentor, mapped the route to many of my "ahas" about teaching writing;

- Tom Kish, who in spite of major transplant surgery, never had a sense-of-humor transplant and provided illustrations for my seminars and sketches to be adapted for the final artwork here;

- Barbara Anderson, senior editor at St. Martin's, who liked the manuscript (bless her!) and edited it with enduring—and endearing—cooperation and skill.

- Marian Lizzi, senior editor at St. Martin's, who also enriched the first edition with her spirit and skill as assistant editor then; and who, with her hallmark grace, capably guided this revised edition to completion. Indeed, I've been twice blessed with her manner and her talent.

- Family and friends, who have been my unconditional well-wishers.

Introduction
Why I Wrote This Book

To a three-year-old child, a crayon in the hand is pure power and enjoyment. Eagerly and effortlessly that youngster scribbles an imprint for the world to see. Yet by the time that child is an adult, and the crayon is replaced by pen, pencil, or computer, the sight of a blank page or blank screen is likely to provoke terror and helplessness.

When and where did so many of us learn to dislike, and even fear, an activity that was once natural and fun? Chances are, it was the moment writing became associated with being graded and judged. Most likely, this happened in school—where, unwittingly, early instruction stressed perfection rather than growth; where misguided teaching sought to correct and eliminate every error at once instead of encouraging experimentation and learning through mistake-making; where to collaborate with another was not only discouraged but often viewed as cheating; where the goal was to impress the teacher by the paper's length—not its message.

No wonder so many of us began to hate writing. Dutifully corrected by well-intentioned teachers, each paper punctured our self-esteem. But, like it or not, we learned to write—for the world of school, that is: Use big words, fill lots of pages, impress the teacher.

But writing in the business world demands different skills—skills not necessarily learned in school. In school we wrote for the teacher only. In the workplace we write for broader audiences with varying needs and expectations. And our business audience is far less patient about wading through our inch-thick reports or reading between the lines for our point. All too often the business writer confuses the goal of business writing with the goal of school writing. In business we write to get a job done, a problem resolved, an action recommended or approved. In school we write to impress the teacher with our display of knowledge and vocabulary.

While this book does not concern itself with school writing, it is adamant about overcoming its legacy. One goal here, then, as in my seminars and private consulting, is to help business writers discard an impoverished view of writing that originated in school and to enlighten them about what works—and won't—in the workplace. The book focuses on the attributes found in the best business writing and on the principles we can follow to make these qualities our own.

A second goal is to remind business writers that although writing well is often challenging, it can just as often be comfortable. Rediscovering that fact will help us once again write effortlessly and emphatically.

Three premises energize this book and my workshops. And these premises are strongly supported by considerable and reputable research into how writing is best learned:

1. We learn to write by writing, often by playful practice. That's why the book is filled with exercises for you to try.

2. We learn to write by discussing our writing with others, by trying it out and getting feedback. That's why sample memos have been included for you to compare with the versions you draft. It's my way of providing feedback, even if only indirectly.

3. We learn to write by groping uncomfortably for a time without fear of reprisal. That's another benefit of the book: You can read and experiment and mess up and try again—in privacy and at leisure.

Enjoy the book. It's different from others that claim you'll learn to write better by just reading about how to do so. Reading alone doesn't make you a better writer. Writing makes you a better writer. So I invite you to interact with the book. Practice and experiment. Try new ways of approaching your business writing. You'll soon find what works best for you, and, I hope, you'll regain that childhood sense of power and ease whenever you find yourself in front of your computer screen or with pen and paper in hand

Part 1   What This Book Can Do for You

Scribendo disces scribere. "*You learn to write by writing.*"
Samuel Johnson

1

From Procrastination to Power: Writing Painlessly and Well

Good writing is good business. Bad writing isn't. To be successful in sales, marketing, finance, engineering, law, personnel, and in virtually every field, you need to write well. In fact, your business writing can serve as persuasive evidence of your competence, your personality, your management style. It's as plain and simple—and frightening—as that.

And, undoubtedly, that fright (those panicky waves in your brain that light out in all directions each time you have to write) has put this edition in your hands. I wrote it as I did the first edition, to do away with your discomfort, to demystify writing and editing, to help you write easily and well. While I can't promise that you'll finish the book loving to write, I do promise that you'll hate writing less—and distribute a better memo, letter, or report as a result of using this practical guide. Whether you are writing an e-mail to a coworker or a proposal to an international client, this book will help.

It offers up-to-date examples and answers, and because it's arranged in units, you can pick it up, do a little work, put it down, and return to it later without having to start over. It doesn't treat improving your written work as if it were a moral issue; nor does it assume that the fate of the world hinges upon your perfect prose. But, with wit and wisdom, it does encourage you and show you how to write better. It will sustain you from your first to your final draft.

For more than twenty years, in one-on-one consultations, in seminars and talks, and in published articles, I've worked to help clients be competent in and feel confident about their writing. Clients who admit their negative attitude about the task. Clients who get stuck at the sight of a blank page or screen. Clients who are disorganized and fuzzy about what to write and what tone to take. Clients who are wordy because they don't know how not to be. Clients who retreat behind a desk in embarrassment—and anger—after their manager has red-penned their grammatical and mechanical errors and, possibly, their career.

If these clients and their writing sound familiar, you've found the book you need. Its advice, anecdotes, and exercises have proven successful in corporate classrooms across the globe and have improved the business writing of countless clients. And those results have encouraged me to encourage you in this newly updated edition.

2
Where to Begin to Improve

How can you begin to improve your writing?

1. Accept that you have to write, for visibility, credibility, promotion. In fact, business people spend an average of 30 percent of their work time writing.

2. Dispel these myths:

   - **Having more words is better.** Consider your office desk and computer. Are your IN boxes and OUT boxes stacked with documents that attempt to sound impressive and important but are filled with dead words and redundant expressions? It's easy to find pages of long-windedness and disorganization—remnants, perhaps, from misguided teaching that emphasized big words and lengthy phrases. People worry that if something is simply stated it can't be intelligent. So they write "pursuant to our agreement" instead of "as we agreed" and "in the normal course of our procedure" rather than "normally."

     But having more words is *not* better. Quantity does not equal quality. In fact, it usually achieves the reverse. Verbiage is inherently inefficient. And the resulting lack of clarity ends up costing companies much—in dollars, wasted hours, and frustration.

   - **Correct writing is good writing.** Ask workers and managers if their reports are well written. Whether they say yes or no, they will likely base their opinion on grammatical considerations—subject-verb agreement, correct verb tenses, whether there are split infinitives and sentence fragments. Certainly usage and the accepted mechanics of written English *are* important. But just because something is written correctly doesn't mean it's written effectively. The next time you read a memo or report, ask yourself: Is it interesting, engaging, clever, concise, logical, easy to follow? Good writing is all of these—and more.

- **Business writing is not creative writing.** Some writing tasks are more routine than others, requiring, perhaps, less creativity. But other writing tasks—such as answering complaints and dealing appropriately with sticky, irksome, or negative situations—require your creative energies to get the results you want. Business writing at its best is a form of problem solving and calls for fresh thinking, imagination, and original, clear language.

3 Believe you *can* improve. Good writers are made, not born.

4. Practice, using some useful techniques.

5. Listen to good advice. Read on!

3
Qualities of Powerful Writing

Just what *is* good business writing? Exactly how do you spot it? *What* makes a memo memorable? Consider these qualities, which will assuredly keep your writing healthy.

Qualities of Powerful Writing

Sense of Audience	Anticipates reader's needs
Right Tone	Is even-tempered
Informative Content	Has substance—says something
Movement	Goes somewhere and has a sense of order
Helpful Format	Looks good on the page, is easy to read, scan, and retrieve information from
Detail	Uses concrete, selective, precise words
Voice	Sounds like one human being talking to another; has a strong, credible imprint of the writer; characterizes the writer; makes reader believe
Originality	Says something new *or* something old in a new way
Rhythm	Sounds effortless, natural
Good Mechanics	Observes conventions of spelling, punctuation, and usage; uses enlightened control by knowingly and occasionally bending the rules

---

Rank the following three samples according to the Qualities of Powerful Writing. Identifying the poor, the passing, the practically perfect—and what makes each so—should be easy.

Version #1

TO: All Employees Who Are Paid Monthly

FROM: The Payroll Department

RE: Your October Paychecks

Regretfully we are writing to advise each of you that have recently signed up for the direct deposit of your paychecks and those of you who have previously been having their pay directly deposited that the arrangement of which we wrote in our September memo is not yet in effect. (Copies of this memo are available upon written request, directed to this office.) What we expected to have happened by the close of the present month will not take place, due to unanticipated technicalities of both an electronic and bureaucratic nature. If you are enrolled already in the direct deposit program for your paycheck, please be advised that we will be unable to have your pay directly deposited to your bank or other type of financial institution according to the schedule we had announced in our earlier communication, mentioned above. If you have not yet enrolled in this program, but were planning to do so at your earliest convenience, be advised that you should do with your paycheck as you were previously accustomed to.

This decision was made to facilitate a problem-free transition from the former system in use to a new system, which promises to expedite the speed with which your monthly earnings become available for meeting your financial needs and requirements of whatever nature. We strongly felt the need to extend the trial prenotification period to a second month was essential as the potential existed that certain wire transfers would be processed unsuccessfully if we went "live" with our automatic deposit plan in a precipitous fashion. Rest assured, however, that each monthly paid employee will, by one channel or another, receive their expected compensation.

We deeply regret any inconvenience this may have caused you, however, we are confident that all the technicalities mentioned above will be laid to rest in a short time frame, and that those of you who are enrolled in the direct deposit program will have your checks directly deposited by the close of the month of November, at the worst, December.

Thank you for your patience as we implement this new and exciting program. If you disagree with our policy, or if you have any questions or comments, you should of course feel perfectly free to contact one of our trained payroll specialists at extension 5432. We will be happy to meet your needs in whatever ways we can do so.

Rank

☐ Poor

☐ Passing

☐ Practically perfect

Version #2

TO: All Employees Who Are Paid Monthly

FROM: The Controller's Office

RE: Direct Deposit of Payroll

Regretfully I am writing to inform those of you who have recently signed up for direct deposit of payroll and for those employees who previously have been having their pay directly deposited that we will be unable to have your pay automatically deposited at your bank or financial institution for the October 25 payroll.

Each monthly paid employee will, however, receive a paycheck as was the case for September. This decision was made to ensure a smooth transition to this new system. I felt the need to extend the trial prenotification period to a second month was essential as the potential existed that certain wire transfers would be made inaccurately if we went "live" with the automatic deposit in October.

I apologize for the inconvenience this may cause you. However, we are confident that all of the kinks will be worked out in October and all automatic deposits of payroll will occur with the November 25 payroll.

Rank

☐ Poor

☐ Passing

☐ Practically perfect

Version #3

TO: Employees Enrolled in the Direct Deposit Plan

FROM: The Payroll Department

RE: Direct Deposit Delayed Until November

We're sorry. In September we announced our plan to deposit your October paycheck directly in your bank. But we need to postpone this until November, to ensure that all the wire transfers can be performed swiftly and accurately.

So on October 25th our old procedure will still be in effect. You'll need to pick up your paycheck and deposit it yourself.

We regret the delay. Thanks for your patience!

Rank
- ☐ Poor
- ☐ Passing
- ☐ Practically perfect

Compare your assessment of the previous samples to this one.

	Version #1	*Version #2*	*Version #3*
Sense of Audience	• Ignores reader's need to get information quickly	• Has sense of and respect for reader's time	• Keeps memo brief in honor of reader's needs
Right Tone	• Overly dramatic and formal	• Even-tempered	• Even-tempered
Informative Content	• Says something, but takes forever and includes more than reader needs	• Has key information	• Contains just what reader needs to know
Movement	• Crawls slowly from point to point	• Long sentences block quick reading. Though wordy, has a sense of order	• Moves quickly from point to point telling reader what's changed and why
Helpful Format	• Opening paragraphs too long	• Short paragraphs work, long sentences don't	• Attractively short, to the point
Detail	• Overly reliant on businessese phrases, complicated language	• Less businessese than in Version #1	• No wasted words
Voice	• Sounds too formal, stilted; trying too hard, pretentious	• Less pretentious than Version #1	• Conversational, genuine-sounding
Originality	• None! Total dependence on overused, stock, stilted language	• Words like "kink" and "live" enliven the writing	• Reliance on own, simple vocabulary
Rhythm	• Sounds staged	• Long sentences detract from easy rhythm	• Nicely mixes sentence lengths and types
Good Mechanics	• Some major flaws	• No glaring errors	• Adheres to conventions
Rank	✔ Poor	✔ Passing	✔ Practically perfect

Even in a commonplace memo about direct deposit, it's not difficult to spot and differentiate bad writing from better. But recognizing what's inherent in powerful writing is one thing; achieving it, quite another. So let's continue our trek toward that goal.

Part 2   Getting the Writing Going

Just get it down on paper, and then we'll see what to do with it.
editor Maxwell Perkins's advice to a novelist

4
Overcoming Page Fright

S cene 1: *Your mouth gets dry. Your palms sweat. The muscles in your legs and neck begin to twitch. Your heart rate accelerates. You get up, pour yourself another cup of coffee, poke about your papers, and then begin to cross out, rip up, swear. Or, you stare at the empty screen defiantly facing you, type in a few words, delete them, press more keys, and start all over again.*

Why? You have to write. Not necessarily something monumental like next year's market plan or your yearly self-assessment. A 150-word memo, for many, is enough to instigate a full-fledged case of page fright.

Scene 2: "The purpose of this memo . . ." (*No, that's a lousy opening.*)
"It has come to my attention that . . ." (*Yuk! That's even worse.*)
"You must consider . . ." (*Rats! Sounds as if I'm giving orders here. I'd better start again.*)
". . ." (*I'm blank! I just can't get started!*)

Do these scenes sound familiar? For many of you these paralyzing moments repeat themselves each time you start to write, flashing a red light and blocking your ability to draft words productively and quickly.

Even if you readily acknowledge the need to write, actually generating your correspondence may not happen quite so easily. Understandably.

Victor Hugo, author of *Les Misérables*, forced himself to write by disrobing and giving his clothing to his valet with strict instructions that it not be returned *until* he had written the allotted pages. Demosthenes took another tack: He shaved half his head, thus forcing himself to remain inside—to write—until he could reappear without shame in public. (Today he'd appear perfectly normal in public, head half shaven!)

While your procrastination may not be so dramatic as either of theirs, it is nonetheless to be reckoned with. For writing is an amazingly complex act that requires several, often conflicting skills. To write well, then, it's helpful to understand these varying and sometimes opposing skills, and to recognize that there is more than one path to effective business writing.

Two skills most commonly in conflict are the natural ability to generate ideas and the natural tendency to edit those ideas the moment they appear on paper or screen (if not sooner!). These two skills often get in the way of each other—largely because the editor in your head is a ruthless tyrant, unsympathetic to your struggle, and because the natural writing process seems to involve your moving back and forth among the stages of composing: incubating ideas, then generating them, crossing out, stopping, planning, reviewing, moving forward, stopping, crossing out, reviewing, generating . . .

To generate easily and quickly requires freedom. Freedom from the pressure of a critical editor who is all too ready (and able) to tell you to change your ideas or spell your words right. Freedom from worry over how you sound as you draft. Freedom from concern over the correctness of your punctuation in the early stages of your writing.

Yet to write concisely, clearly, and powerfully requires an objective, even relentless editor who demands for you to not just get your ideas across but also to write them correctly. Even for the professional writer, that's a lot to ask.

How, then, in this conflicting process, can you accomplish good writing? Read on!

5
Getting Started: Strategies That Work

If you struggle to get those first words down (because your critical editor won't let you generate before criticizing), the following advice may help.

- Assume a "can do" attitude. Don't wait for the muse. Stop being your own worst enemy. You *can* write.

- Give yourself permission to say it the wrong way before you say it the right way. The big problem people have when they sit down to write is wanting to express themselves perfectly the first time. While that does happen occasionally, the truth is that good writing is *rewriting*. Focus your initial energy on capturing all the content and ideas you believe belong in your final draft. Be concerned with *what* you have to say, not *how* you're saying it. Remember, being too critical of yourself early in your writing can get you hung up. Trust the process. It doesn't have to start out right as long as it ends up that way.

- Give yourself a deadline—say ten or twenty minutes—for writing that first, fast, zero draft. Write nonstop, trying not to separate the writing from the thinking at this point. You will find that the act of moving your pencil or pen across the paper, or your fingers across the keyboard, will activate your thinking—much more so than staring out the window or up at the ceiling waiting for the right words to come. Moving words across a page or screen, even if they aren't the precise words you want, will help you arrive at the right ones. The hand, eye, and brain need practice working together. Don't put the total burden on your brain to think it out *before* it reaches the paper. In fact, the writing will help you clarify your ideas and help you discover new ones. As one famous writer put it, "How do I know what I think until I see what I say?" Nonstop writing will help you overcome resistance to writing. Aim for quantity, not quality, at first. The value of stopwatch writing is in getting started easily, not in what you first produce.

Here are specific deadline writing techniques for getting your first, fast, zero draft done—and for inviting fresh insights to enliven your workday writing, insights that often elude you when you use only an outline to get started. Even if your projects are purely quantitative, getting-started techniques will help breathe life into your writing—especially if you feel bored by and unconnected to your topic and/or burdened by having to document it.

1. **Begin with a bogus first sentence.** It doesn't matter if it's as trite as "Here's what I think . . . ," "I'm writing this to persuade you to . . . ," or "What I'm trying to say is . . . ." The value of the bogus sentence is that it gets you to the point(s) you need to make. Like training wheels on a bicycle, the bogus sentence starter can be removed later.

2. **Begin by talking what you want to write.**

   - Use a tape recorder or dictating machine. (Many microcassette models are available, some of which are voice activated.) Close your eyes and imagine yourself taking dictation from the voice inside your head that knows what you're trying to say. This way, and at this stage in the writing, you won't be distracted by trying to spell every word right. While this method of getting started may feel uncomfortable at first, practice will bring about ease. In other words, don't try it once and then give up.

   - Ask a colleague to help you loosen the logjam. Often just talking about what you have to write will help you clarify your idea and recover a "can do" state of mind.

3. **Begin anywhere.** Ezra Pound once said, as a metaphor for approaching writing, "When you're building a table, it doesn't matter what leg you put on first—just as long as you end up with four." The same maxim applies to your writing. If your first sentence is stalling you, start with another part of your report or memo.

4. **Try a nontraditional outline.** This technique, known as mind mapping, webbing, or clustering, is a fast, nonlinear way to get words on paper.

Those who find it difficult to make a traditional outline before writing applaud this method. After all, not all of us know what we want to say before we've written it. Mind mapping is like playing word association. It allows you to see patterns and relationships in your subject. Here's how to do it.

- Start with a key word or phrase in the center of your paper or screen. (If you generate on the computer, you can use a software program called Inspiration or download one called MindMapper directly from the Internet.)

- Then quickly let words spill and radiate outward. The randomness with which you started will shift, and you'll experience a sense of direction within seconds.

Try this technique as a substitute for formal outlining. It will help you recall details and fuel you when you feel disorganized by helping you quite literally see relationships.

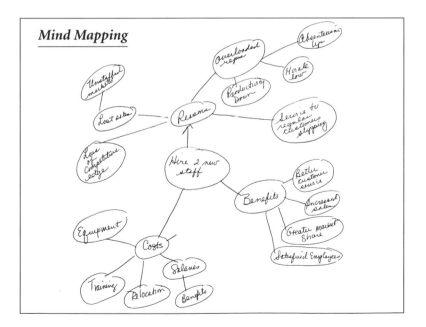

5. **Write a news article.** Play the journalist and write your memo as though you were answering the who, what, when, where, why, and how questions. Then give it an engaging headline as your subject (Re:) line.

6. **Doodle.** Often images play a productive role in thinking. As with mind mapping, an image contains a graphic, holistic representation of ideas—a gestalt: a picture. Although images are rarely expressed in published writings, they are a private source of inspiration. As such, they can provide a starting point for writing.

   The priority of images in the development of scientific ideas can be exemplified by Charles Darwin's recurrent image of the irregularly branching tree of nature. This image foreshadowed his theory of evolution, and it was through it that he was able to express his thoughts about natural selection. Darwin's image, in its recurring form, can be found in his *First Notebook*.

   While you may not be working on so profound a theory, doodling is a useful place to start. See if you can pictorially express the concept(s) you want your reader to grasp.

7. **Write nonstop.** Take ten to twenty minutes, whatever time you can spare without interruption, and just write. Don't pause to cross out, correct, criticize. Don't stop to stare or think. In fact, don't separate the writing from the thinking. Give yourself a bogus first sentence such as "I'm writing to tell you that . . ." or "I want you to know that . . ." or a statement or opinion about your subject. The object of this brief writing marathon is not to create fine writing the first time around but to make you more fluent and free. The fine-tuning ought to—and will—come later. What if you get stuck, stopped, stalled? Just continue writing about your mind being stuck or not being able to write. Or you can just write the same word over and over again. Trust the process. It's warm-up writing. You may even find some gems you can take from your nonstop draft.

8. **Capture first impressions.** Put down quickly, as with nonstop writing, all thoughts and reactions you happen to have about the topic. These first impressions often open doors to important insights you might miss

were you to approach the writing first from straightforward, analytic thinking.

9. **Admit biases.** Uncover your opinions and preferences before you do any careful thinking. This exercise will help you explore the differences between your indefensible beliefs and authentic arguments—an important distinction if you are writing to persuade.

10. **Write dialogue.** When you discover conflicting or confusing ideas or feelings, have them talk to or argue with each other on paper. Creating a dialogue may help you produce reasons or reach decisions. Part of the power comes from inviting yourself to write the way you speak. The result is that you produce not merely reasons but also a credible, engaging essay sound, rather than one that is flat or stilted.

11. **Try stream-of-consciousness thinking.** Write out the narrative going on in your mind. Although a slow process, it is useful when your topic is confusing or when you find your point of view shifting. This warm-up helps untie the knots in your thinking.

12. **Tell stories.** This technique helps write a recommendation letter or evaluate a person or project. Recall stories, anecdotes, incidents associated with your subject. Write each down, briefly. Each may have a special insight you can build on. What's more, this technique will spare your reader(s) from the dullness characteristic of evaluations. In fact, letters of recommendation work best if they include specific examples.

13. **Vary your audience.** If your audience is intimidating, try writing your first draft to another, more friendly audience. This will serve several purposes. First, you can get started. Second, if you write your first draft to your child or your mother, you'll likely notice important aspects of your report or recommendation that you *wouldn't* have realized if you first wrote directly to your boss.

14. **Vary the writer.** Pretend you're someone else writing about your topic. You'll get beyond the blank screen more quickly and perhaps generate new insights during this early draft.

These methods for generating writing were first developed by Peter Elbow, a noted writing researcher and professor. More about them can be found in his book *Writing with Power*, mentioned in the bibliography.

Your darkest moments needn't come each time you have to write a memo. Instead, clear your throat, turn to the back of an envelope, and trick yourself into an informal, quick start. If that doesn't work, choose from among the other suggestions mentioned in this section. None of the approaches here will increase the amount of time you spend writing; they'll just change the way you spend that time—and the quality of your finished memo.

Part 3 Showcasing Your Ideas and Information Through Organization, Format, and Sentence Structure

"If you have something important to say—please—start at the end."

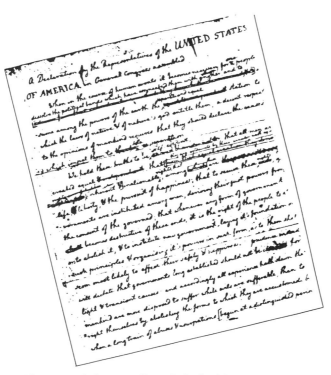

First page of Thomas Jefferson's draft of the Declaration of Independence, with the corrections of John Adams and Benjamin Franklin. (*Courtesy of Library of Congress*)

6
Organizing Your Message

GET TO THE BOTTOM LINE!

Once you've got all your ideas down on paper or screen, the next step is to organize them so they present the most clear, powerful, and persuasive message to your reader(s). Most executives would agree that bottom-lining—summarizing your major point(s) at the outset—is the single most effective (and appreciated) form of organization. Bottom-lining is nothing more—or less—than putting your main point up front as your opening sentence. It's a strategy used by every top journalist, and one that savvy business writers can benefit from, too.

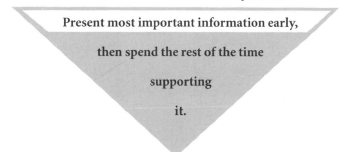

Use Journalism's Inverted Pyramid

Present most important information early,

then spend the rest of the time

supporting

it.

Bottom lines telegraph a variety of messages to readers.

- Some **summarize:**

    The department agreed to allocate an additional $50,000 to the new project and to meet vendors who can support the 3Q due date. Here are the details of the meeting.

- Others **exhort a reader to action:**

    My visit on June 28 to the Michigan market revealed two back-order problems needing your immediate response.

- Some **announce policy:**

    To accommodate those of you on flextime, the cafeteria will now be open from 6 A.M. to 3 P.M.

- Other bottom lines **recommend**. For example:

TO:	John C. McIntyre	**DATE:**	
FROM:	Jean Smith	**COPIES:**	
SUBJECT:	**Recommendation to Sponsor Adult Soccer Springfield, MA**		

Sponsoring Springfield Adult Soccer (SAS) (see enclosed) will afford us the benefits we derived through last year's sponsorship, and I heartily endorse our participation.

Three Benefits to Sponsorship

- **Leverage** with our accounts in the district through product ads, tickets, etc.
- **Brands exposure** to more than 30,000 attendees
- **Affordability** – With little money available from the district, Account Specific funds can be tapped. Collectively, this is a sponsorship program we can afford.

Background: What Is Springfield's Adult Soccer Festival?

Briefly, the SAS Festival is a 32-game adult soccer tournament that has attracted over 30,000 people each year of its two-year history. The 32 teams will participate in this four-week tournament during March at Behanna Stadium outside Springfield.

Your Recommendation, Please

Look over the enclosed package and let me know by Tuesday, 5 January if you agree that this sponsorship is worthwhile and I'll start "the ball moving." Call/Audix me your decision.

Thanks!

■ Bottom lines can also **seek the reader's approval**. For example:

TO: Mr. T. Murphy   DATE:

FROM: D.K. Mountner   COPIES:

RE: **Pricing Analysis Supports Status Quo**

Region responses to our June pricing analysis recommend no change in price at this time but rather to bring prices in line with corporate guidelines during the next price increase. I agree and request your approval. Attached for reference are responses from the various regions.

Background: Steps in Our Analysis

In late June we forwarded an analysis of prices versus those of the competition. This analysis concluded that our prices were generally competitive and not negatively influencing our business. Prices were in compliance with corporate guidelines, though some small variations existed. We asked the regions to review the analysis and recommend a course of action.

Recommendation: No Change Now and Why

We recommend no change in prices at this time but will attempt to bring all prices in line with guidelines at the time of the next price increase. Our decision took into account the following:

• Variations are small and not hurting our business;

• A change now just prior to another price increase could cause serious retailer problems;

• The earnings impact is minimal, at $100M for the balance of the year.

Assuming your agreement, I will advise the regions to hold prices now but to bring them into line during the next increase.

HOW TO TELL A BOTTOM-LINE STATEMENT
FROM A PURPOSE STATEMENT

Sometimes it's difficult to decide which part of your letter or memo or report is the bottom line. Just keep in mind that a bottom line *summarizes* your message or explains what action you advise taking or what action/response you hope the person reading your message will take. A bottom-line statement gets the reader to think or say, "Oh!" versus "So . . . what!" The "oh/so . . . what" test lets you know if you've begun with a strong bottom line or started instead with once-upon-a-time background or explanation.

A bottom line is never a purpose statement, which is an opening sentence that tells the reader what the *purpose* of the memo is but does not summarize it. Here are some examples of purpose statements:

Purpose Statement: The following are comments heard from retailers and consumers, and my observations of industry and competitive performance.

While this opening sentence tells the reader what the purpose of the memo is—to relate comments and observations—it does not summarize them. In fact, such an opening statement merely repeats what your subject line has already said. That repetition is not particularly useful or effective.

The next examples do no better.

Purpose Statement: This represents a response to your letter regarding the expansion of our promotion in Wisconsin.

Purpose Statement: John, this is a recap of the Shelf-Management Program presented to W. D. Corporation on 2 June.

Purpose Statement: The following is a summary of my recent market visit.

Purpose Statement: This paper will recommend the action we should take against the competition.

Purpose statements are not the most effective way to start a memo. Bottom-line statements are far more powerful and forceful. To demonstrate, read the following example, which begins with a purpose statement. Then read the example again, but this time omit the first sentence. See how much more suc-cinct it becomes. Why? It now starts with the bottom line.

Here are two more examples to make my point. Remove the opening pur-pose statement. Again, see how much more direct it becomes when you begin with the bottom line instead.

> The enclosed data compare our status against the competition's. Through the week of 28 June we have lost share in retail sales while our three major competitors have gained. A close look at the data will show our downward slide.

> Enclosed please find attached Draft #3 of our Chug-a-Lug™ National Relaunch Implementation Manual. We need your help to ensure that the information in the attached draft is one hundred percent accurate and up to date.

Since a bottom line is a telegram to your reader, to write a strong one, ask yourself, "What is the most important point I need to make?" Then position that point up front, as shown in these two examples.

Bottom-Lined Memo #1

TO: Dee Boss

FROM: M. Happy

RE: Success at W. D. Corporation

Dee, our Shelf-Management Program gained us the competitive edge at W. D. Corporation on 2 June. They approved our recommended configuration and believe it will grow their sales and profits. Here are the details of the meeting:

- accepted configuration, with stipulation we present the program at division level

- reduced peg by one third

- added 30 linear feet of shelving

- requested Space-Management resources for item layout and selection

- will evaluate in six months to determine effect on business and the brands

Bottom-Lined Memo #2

TO: All District #777 Wholesalers

RE: **Offsetting Competition's New Product Introduction**

To neutralize the introduction of the competition's new Widget Wonder into the marketplace in April, we need your help. We ask that you each develop an aggressive action plan.

Place particular emphasis on

- distributing our four best widgets: the 1100, 1200, 1400, and the Super Widget, particularly in chain accounts

- ensuring dominant shelf space in each account

- placing advertisements

- ensuring that your sales force maintains a strong call frequency meeting daily objectives.

Please provide your detailed action plan to me by March 8. If you have questions, please call. Thank you.

Regards,

Emma Bottomliner
Emma Bottomliner
District Manager, #777

BOTTOM-LINING EXERCISES

As you try the following exercises, keep this bottom line in mind!

Don't bury the message.

Here are three memos whose bottom lines could be more prominent. Try revising them, and while you're at it, make your subject line more informative.

Memo #1 First Draft

TO: All District #777 Wholesalers

RE: Cisco Quick Marts

Recently I met with Don Kemsak, marketing director of Cisco Quick Marts. Don has authorized our family 12-pack displays starting August 6 and continuing through September 4.

Don has approved the use of our new slogan banners. To take advantage of this opportunity, I suggest you use our full array of Labor Day decorative banners. Also, Don has stated that he prefers either block or circular displays in his Cisco Quick Marts.

Work with your individual store managers in order to secure the proper floor space and utilize the banner material available.

If you have any questions regarding this great opportunity in your Cisco Quick Marts, please give me a call.

Thank you and good selling.

Notta Bottomliner
Notta Bottomliner
District Manager, #777

Here's one bottom-lined revision to compare with yours.

Memo #1 Revision

TO: All District #777 Wholesalers

RE: Cisco Quick Marts Wants Our Displays

Don Kemsak, marketing director of Cisco Quick Marts, has authorized the building of our 12-pack displays in his stores from August 6 to September 4. Further, he

- has approved our decorative slogan banners and

- prefers either block or circular displays.

You can use the full array of our decorative material once you've secured floor space from your individual store managers.

Thanks—and good selling.

Emma Bottomliner
Emma Bottomliner
District Manager, #77

Here's another to try to improve.

Memo #2 First Draft

MEMORANDUM

TO: Ed Ditter   DATE: 2 May

SUBJECT: Marketing Meeting   FROM: Ike Cantwright

Way back last November when we first got around to planning
this meeting, I thought I would be back from the National Sales
Conference—it's going to be in the Bahamas this year, rather
than Topeka—and I'm looking forward to getting a good tan,
too. Well, anyway, I figured I could easily be back in town by the
18th, but now I've got to stop off in St. Louis on the way back, to
talk to some of our people about the Satellite Project. So I'm not
sure now whether I will be back by the 18th, or even the 19th.
I'm just not sure how bad the situation is there. So what about
the 20th? I've tried reaching you on the phone, but your assistant
couldn't speak to your schedule, so I figured I'd better send you
this. Let me know what's best for you. Of course, when I get in
I'll be brushing sand off me.
Know any good restaurants there?

Here's one bottom-lined revision to compare with yours. While it maintains the informal sound of the original draft, it no longer meanders needlessly.

Memo #2 Revision

MEMORANDUM

TO: Ed Ditter   DATE: 2 May

SUBJECT: Date Change/Marketing Meeting   FROM: Ike Cantwright

How is the 20th for our meeting? An unplanned stopover in St. Louis to discuss the Satellite Project keeps me from getting back earlier, as originally planned. By then I'll have all the sand brushed off me from the National Sales Conference in the Bahamas. Leave a response on my VMX. Thanks.

Help! What is the bottom line here? To offer thanks or to get work out more efficiently? You decide. Then rewrite.

Memo #3 First Draft

FROM:	Patricia Brasher
To:	Art Proofing Group
CC:	
BCC:	
SUBJECT:	Proofing

I want to thank you all for filling in during my absence. I appreciate all of your help. I know that this added responsibility has caused you to rearrange your schedules, but please know that your help is greatly appreciated.

I want to share the following information with you. I've identified just a few areas where we can improve our efficiency.

1) I would like all artwork prioritized as follows:

> color keys/color separations
> thermals
> POS
> rule copy

2) It is crucial to pull art from the bottom of the bin, not the top. The things on the bottom have been there the longest and should be looked at first.

3) I ask that you not separate art according to brand. I want you to proof art in the order that it appears in the box. I truly understand how this may make things flow easier for the proofer (all of the art for one brand is together). However, separating art this way may cause some pieces of art to sit in the box for 3–4 days, as opposed to 1–2 days. I'm much more concerned with accuracy than with speed when you are proofing.

I thank you for your cooperation and help.

Here's another bottom-lined version to compare with yours.

Memo #3 Revision

FROM:	Patricia Brasher
TO:	Art Proofing Group
CC:	
BCC:	
SUBJECT:	Poofing . . . er, Proofing Guidelines!

These three suggestions should help us get through this crunch time efficiently.

- Prioritize all artwork as follows:
    1. color keys/color separations
    2. thermals
    3. POS
    4. rule copy

- Pull art from the bottom of the bin, not the top. The things on the bottom have been there longest and should be looked at first.

- Proof art in the order that it appears in the box. Do not separate art according to brand. While separating may make things flow easier for the proofer, it may cause some pieces to sit in the box for three or four days, as opposed to one or two days. Let's make accuracy rather than speed our goal.

Thank you all for filling in during my absence. I appreciate your willingness to rearrange schedules with the added responsibilities.

Patricia Brasher

WHEN NOT TO BOTTOM-LINE

Bottom-lining places your message—your main point—up front in your memo. And even when you have bad or disappointing news to send, most readers prefer a direct approach. A circuitous route is often viewed as patronizing and phony. On rare occasions, however, you may prefer a less-than-bottom-lined approach. For instance, when you are writing to a reader with a strong negative bias toward what you're recommending or requesting, or when you need to tell your boss that one of his or her special projects (such as a budget cut) just won't work. In these instances, instead of placing your message in your first sentence, you may want to start with a general point, a point of common ground. From there you can draw your reader through a presentation of your points, finally stating your precise request or recommendation toward the end of the memo. Such a buffered approach offers a psychological as well as a logical appeal. In such difficult circumstances, though, a meeting rather than a memo may work better. Knowing when *not* to write is as valuable as knowing when to—or not to—bottom-line.

Examples of buffered memos to a reader with a strong negative bias:

Buffered Memo #1

TO: Boss

FROM: Jess Mitigate

SUBJECT: Potential Impact of Cost Reductions

I've met with key managers in our group to discuss the budget advisory requiring a 12 percent reduction in personnel costs. In engineering, this reduction equates to five engineers and two technicians.

We felt the head-count cuts needed to meet this objective would jeopardize reaching several of our goals, namely

Project	Estimated Financial Impact Over 24 Months
• development of an enhanced wave-soldering workstation to improve by 25 percent our circuit-board quality	$2.8M
• reengineering of power supply and CRT for standard product to eliminate excessively high failure rate	$1.5M
• component engineering analysis on four highest-volume product lines—to improve yield and reduce component count	$825,000

Because these goals represent three of the most important strategic activities planned over the next two years, we'd like to revisit them with you to validate their strategic importance before we act on the personnel reductions.

We are available Thursday or Friday to meet with you.

Buffered Memo #2

TO: Dave Stevenson

FROM: Les Thomas

SUBJECT: A Second Chance?

Bob Beatty let me know that my request for a transfer to your new sales group has not been approved. Naturally, I'm disappointed, but based on the information you had to make that decision, I can see how you concluded there was no match. There are, however, several experiences and accomplishments during my years at OBC Corporation that could be of value and that you may not have been aware of. For example,

- while I was product marketing manager, I developed a strategy that successfully increased market share by 15 points over a 12-month period in four diverse ethnic markets; also

- I managed the development and rollout of three new products and exceeded financial objectives by 12 percent.

I'd appreciate spending half an hour with you to discuss how these and other experiences might complement the new sales group's efforts. I'll call in a few days to check your availability.

Thanks.

ORGANIZING THE REST OF THE DOCUMENT

Bottom-lining gets your message up front: "Hire the additional staff," "Sales were the best ever," "Our ad campaign worked beyond our hopes." Ninety-nine percent of your reports, memos, and letters ought to start at the end; that is, your bottom line should be stated in the first sentence, making it easy for busy readers to understand what you want to say. But then you still have to figure out how to organize the *rest* of the document. The following patterns of organization can help support your points and help you link one to the next.

Order, indeed, is important. And you have a range of choices to create that order. What you need to ask yourself is this: "Which arrangement—or combination of arrangements—will make my memo most readable, memorable, and persuasive to my audience?"

ARRANGING IDEAS IN AN EFFECTIVE LOGICAL ORDER

Each of the following patterns has valid uses—together and in combination. Wisely chosen, each invites your writing to flow naturally, even predictably, from your opening statement to your close. The result? Your readers will appreciate being able to process your points easily!

- A **chronological** pattern is most useful when you are recounting a sequence of events, as in a progress/status report or when describing a step-by-step procedure.

- A **spatial** pattern relies on spatial references rather than on a time frame around which to organize your document. Engineers, scientists, and architects find a spatial pattern useful when describing a mechanism, a molecule, or a mall.

- An **order-of-importance** pattern suggests to your reader what is most critical, what is least. Such a pattern assigns significance where you want your

reader to see it. Recommendations, proposals, even trip re
read more easily using such a pattern.

- A **pro-and-con** pattern serves well when you must presen
argument. Sometimes called an *advantages-and-disadvantag*
organization allows your readers to see all sides of an issue.
used in a recommendation, this pattern lets your readers see how thoroughly you've researched your material.

- A **cause-and-effect** pattern is useful for several writing tasks: presenting a
logical argument; describing a process; explaining a phenomenon; and pre-
dicting what might occur in the future.

- A **compare-and-contrast** pattern, like the pro-and-con pattern, allows
readers to see similarities and differences as you make your case for or
against something.

- A **category and/or listing** pattern has distinct advantages in your business
prose. For instance, if you're recommending a new hire, you may want to
categorize or list the candidate's strengths. If you're writing a performance
review, you may want to categorize major accomplishments—for instance:
Sales, Cost Savings, Customer Relations, Quality Control, etc.

- A **problem-to-solution** pattern offers yet another means for you to proceed logically in a recommendation or proposal. A variation of this pattern
lets you eliminate several solutions in favor of the one you are proposing.

7

Formatting Ideas to Clarify Your Message

WRITE HEADLINES THAT HELP

Now that you've realized the value of placing your bottom line—your key point—in the opening sentence (or very close to it!), where else can you clarify your message and support your bottom line? An obvious, yet often overlooked place is your subject line. Along with your bottom line statement it is prime real estate in your document!

Most business writing contains a subject line. Use yours not merely to state the broad topic area but to get your reader's attention and to move your reader's mind in the direction of your thinking. It is your opportunity to provide your reader the outcome—or the summary of your thinking about the topic—to put the appropriate spin on the situation. Again, play the journalist: Turn your subject line into a headline. And remember, a good headline can stand alone.

If you write "Business Climate" as your subject line, what will differentiate that memo from a stack of others already written with the same subject line?

Use **headlines** instead of subject lines. Think of yourself as selling your memo to the *Wall Street Journal* or the *New York Times*. You've got to *interest* and intrigue your reader. More important, you've got to *tell* your reader something. Headlines do that. Subject lines don't always.

So write . . .

Not a Bland Title,	→	*An Informative One*
Introduction		Our Search for the Holy Grail
Section 2.3		33 Ways to Cut Costs

Not a Bland Title, →	*An Informative One*
Section 1	Why We Should Consider an Additional 4 Percent Reduction
Report from Task Force	Recommendation to Freeze Prices
Quality-Discount Structure	Recommended Increase in Quality Discounts
Pricing Analysis	Pricing Analysis Suggests Status Quo
Market Report	Market Visits Uncover Issues
Winn-Dixie Presentation	Success at Winn-Dixie
Marketing Meeting	Marketing Meeting Schedule Change
Account Information	Two Top Accounts Change Management

You can use headlines in a variety of ways—each one enticing, inviting, and encouraging the reader to find out more.

- Explain.

  How to Increase Productivity
- Use numbers.

  Five Steps to Increase Productivity
- Use an "ing" verb.

  Increasing Your Productivity Easily
- Create a need.

  The Need to Increase Your Productivity
- Use a whole sentence.
  Declarative:

  Increasing Productivity Decreases Costs

  Imperative:

  Increase Productivity Before Our Competitors Do

  Interrogative:

  How Can We Increase Productivity Substantially?

Note: Headlines work best when they contain a verb!

USE "CHUNKING" TO ORGANIZE YOUR THOUGHTS

Because the eye leads the mind, a dense or cluttered page of type often turns the eye away, saying to the reader, "This is too boring or difficult or busy for me to get through." To avoid getting such a reaction from your readers, try formatting your memos and reports so your prose is divided into chunks, each one labeled with a subhead positioned flush left, resumé style that describes or summarizes what the paragraph is about. In other words, break up your information into manageable, and interesting, chunks. These chunks offer your reader a roadmap through your document. And with a roadmap, your reader—and your message points—are less likely to get lost. When you use subheads and chunking, you increase your reader's ability to accomplish the three R's with your information: Read, Remember, Retrieve.

Here are several examples.

Memo #1

TO: Business Effectiveness Team   DATE: 1 August

FROM: Carrie Luffy   COPIES:

RE: **Increase Meeting Results with Planning**

We Need . . .   Your energy, presence, and participation for the upcoming quarterly Business Effectiveness Team (BET) Meeting at the Ritz Carlton 10 September. The focus of the meeting will be on integrating communication, sharing knowledge among projects, and measuring our success.

Objectives . . .
- Promote teamwork and interaction
- Engage group in quality circles
- Communicate
  1. Where are we today?
  2. Where are we headed?
- Share strategic direction
- Celebrate success

A Little Homework, Please . . .   Attached is a meeting matrix for you to gather your ideas and thoughts for the breakout sessions. This is an **"IDA"** session. **Ideas** will be **Developed,** and we'll leave with an **Action** plan.

We will not have dedicated time for phone calls. Therefore, let your constituents know you will be out of the office for the day.

Take Me Out to the Ballgame . . .   BET Bombers will challenge the In-Market group in softball 9 September at 3:30 PM. Whether you want to play, cheer, eat, or get acquainted with your peers, there is an opportunity for everyone! Details will be e-mailed from Coach Davis by end of week. *See you at the ballpark!*

Memo #2

TO:	DATE:
FROM:	COPIES:

SUBJECT: What to Wear When

We've recently observed attire that raises the question (and eyebrows) about what people really feel is acceptable attire at Seymour Sales, Inc. As a result, we've realized a few reminders are in order. This memo is intended to clarify a standard without prescribing what to wear.

Mondays Through Thursdays – Standard Business Attire, Please

Employees should wear clothes suitable for a professional office where customers, clients, vendors, and others visit.

In some areas (for example, the manufacturing floor, laboratories, and maintenance shops), less formal clothing standards have been adopted based on safety and comfort considerations for the type of work to be performed.

Fridays – Relax, It's Business Casual Attire

For several years, Friday has been "dress down day" at Seymour Sales, Inc. But, based on the questions asked—and the attire seen—this practice warrants clarifying. So we have redesignated Friday's dress code as business casual. Since we often have customers visit on Fridays, we need to convey the image that while we are casual about our business attire and perhaps more comfortable on Fridays, we are still an operating business.

Guidelines to Use

These guidelines should help you make judgment calls about what is—or isn't—appropriate.

1. With the exception of arms and Adam's apples, no more skin than is visible the rest of the week at work should become so on Fridays. This includes . . .

    - fashion extremes (low necklines, high hemlines, or midriff-revealing tops);
    - casual shorts (other than knee-length dress shorts);
    - thonged sandals; or
    - ripped (or stained) jeans.

2. Avoid T-shirts, tank tops, clothing made of spandex, sweatshirts, or exercise wear.

If you have doubts about whether an outfit would be considered business casual, it's probably wise to select another.

Memo #3

We'd like to earn your trust—and your business.

WHO WE ARE   Commercial sheetfed printer in Maryland Heights, MO

A specialty shop with maximum sheet size of 20"x26"

Laminating, foil embossing, spot UV

Services include pamphlets, brochures, catalogs, counter cards, posters, leaflets, pocket folders, ad campaign products

ADVANTAGES UNIQUE TO INDUSTRY

- Full service

- Personal attention

- Competitive price

TRY US   We encourage you to let us quote on your current project or even a previous work order to see how competitive we really are. To do so, please fax us at (314) 622-2478.

If you have any questions, please call me at (800) 246-8115.

Thank you for your consideration.

Tom Rohlfing
President
Pinnacle Press

Here are four more before-and-after examples of what chunking can do to improve your business writing.

Memo #4 First Draft

TO: All Employees
FROM: André Preneur, President
RE: Reorganization of the Company

We can all be proud of the fine performance we turned in over the past 36 months. In that period our company grew 400 percent from annual sales of $5 million to our current rate of $20 million. We've managed to grow, and to do it profitably! That's something to be proud of!

So with all these good things happening, you may ask, "Why reorganize?" Well, it's a good question and one I'd like to spend some time on.

Our company is at a critical point in its growth right now. We're about as stretched as we can be—and the requirements for us to continue at the same pace are compounding and dramatically changing at the same time. This is the point at which many companies don't act. They continue the status quo . . . resting on their past accomplishments. They may never, as a result, achieve their rightful place among the finest-performing companies. I hope I speak for each of us when I say, "We don't want that to happen to us."

So what are we attempting to do by reorganizing? We are positioning ourselves for the future—a future with its own unique requirements, just as our start-up period had its unique characteristics and requirements. And because the requirements are changing, we must redeploy our resources into roles best suited to meet the new challenges.

Each of the roles in this organization has significance—so let's not hear any gossip about who outdid whom in the new organization. In my view, all these jobs must be done well for the company to do well. The first job to change is mine. I'll be taking a more active role in planning and business development, and leaving the operating parts of the business to John Derkee. John will assume the role of Executive Vice President, Operations, and will be responsible for Materials, Manufacturing and Processing Engineering, and Facilities. Ray Elder, formerly Production Superintendent, will take over John Derkee's role as Manufacturing Manager. Alice Hawkins, Bob Brady and Ralph Newberger will continue in their positions managing Process Engineering, Materials and Facilities, respectively.

Ray Smith will continue to handle sales. We have hired Don Luddington, who will join us on July 10 as Vice President, Marketing and Sales, reporting to me. This is a new position in which we hope to integrate all customer- and market-related functions. Ray Smith will report to Mr. Luddington.

Also on July 10, Elizabeth Oxford will join us in the newly created position of Director, Research and Development, reporting to me. Dr. Oxford, thoroughly familiar with both our present product and the technological trends of our industry, will provide technical direction to move our company to its next level of growth.

Al Marchetti will continue to serve in the finance function, with additional responsibilities for expansion and capacity planning.

Donald Gelinas, formerly Employee Relations Manager, has been appointed Director of Human Resources. We'll be adding staff to this function, enabling us to develop the programs and systems to retrain our key resources . . . and attract the new ones we'll need to meet our growth plans.

Your managers will discuss with each of you what, if any, changes beyond these I've mentioned may affect you. All I can ask is that you extend the same degree of cooperation in the future as you have in the past. If you do that—we'll succeed.

Memo #4 Revision

TO: All Employees
FROM: André Preneur, President
RE: Reorganization Focuses on Future Growth

PAST PERFORMANCE A PROUD ONE

Our company has performed superbly in the last three years, since our start-up. Here are a few highlights of our performance:

- Sales growth of 400%
- Before-tax profit during start-up period
- Market share of 35% in standard products
- Development of a work force with high potential for growth
- Impressive industry reputation
- Our capability stretched to its limits

NEW FOCUS FOR GROWTH

To position ourselves for the future—and its demanding requirements—we are refocusing our resources on the important tasks for continued growth. These are:

- Devise a sound planning and business development strategy
- Continue operational excellence
- Broaden sales activity to strategic product-marketing approach
- Develop a research and development function to design products for our future
- Improve business controls and management reporting systems
- Develop our human resources to accomplish our objectives

ORGANIZATION CHANGES

Therefore, we are making the following organization changes effective September 1:

Name	From	To	Key Function
André Preneur	President	Pres. & CEO	Planning, Business Development, & Strategy
John Derkee	Manufacturing Manager	Exec. VP, Operations	Manufacturing, Process Engineering, Materials, & Facilities
Donald Luddington	Hired 7/10 from ABO Corp.	VP, Marketing & Sales	Marketing & Sales Strategy, Policy & Execution
Ray Smith	National Sales Manager	Director, Sales	Sales Objectives
Dr. Elizabeth Oxford	Hired 7/10 from XYZ Corp.	Director, Research & Development	New Products & Technologies for Future
Al Marchetti	Director of Finance	Same	Finance, Facility & Capacity Planning
Donald Gelinas	Employee Relations Manager	Director, Human Resources	Total Human Resources Function
Ray Elder	Production Superintendent	Manufacturing Manager	Quality Control

By extending the same degree of cooperation in the future as you have in the past, I'm confident we'll succeed.

Memo #5 First Draft

DATE: Now

TO: All Region V Reps
FROM: O. Raposa
RE: MANAGERS' MEETING

This meeting was to discuss changes in prices, multiscale installations and problems of growth in the industry, reps to be hired for new areas, problems with filling out service reports, complaints about customer service, and a report on the company's health.

New prices will go into effect on 5/18/—. We will then have a new option for customers to use—the 15-day response. This was requested to accommodate the difference between the emergency and the 60-day call.

Bill Bower explained the flow of paperwork involved between placing a multiscale order and installation. The problem: not enough lead time given to the reps. So that you can get in touch with customers before the three-day installation time is upon you, Bill will have the following information supplied to you whenever you are notified of a pending installation:

> Customer's name
> Address
> Phone number

We now have two areas without reps. Bemidji is being covered by Tom Smith until Bob Kelly finishes his training. We hope he'll be in place by the end of the year. The Minneapolis area is being covered for two months by Brad Shipley, on loan from Montana. Thanks to Larry James and Mike Gentry for this loan to help us keep up with our present workloads. Thanks also to Rich David for keeping our customers in two areas happy. I'll be calling on all of you to help as the need arises. Please let me know with as much lead time as you can when you'll be able to help. A new area is being opened in Walker. It is for 40 percent travel, and the sales rep will have to build up the area as well as pick up overloads in other areas.

Memo #5 Revision

DATE: Now

TO: All Region V Reps

FROM: O. Raposa

RE: MANAGERS' MEETING RECAP, 5/18/__

PRICE CHANGES

New prices will go into effect on 5/18/__. We will then have a new option for customers to use—the 15-day response. This was requested to accommodate the difference between the emergency and the 60-day call.

NEW MULTISCALE INSTALLATIONS PROCEDURE

Bill Bower explained the flow of paperwork involved between placing a multiscale order and installation.The problem: not enough lead time given to the reps. So that you can get in touch with customers before the three-day installation time is upon you, Bill will have the following information supplied to you whenever you are notified of a pending installation:

  Customer's name
  Address
  Phone number

GROWING PAINS

We now have two areas without reps.

- Bemidji is being covered by Tom Smith until Bob Kelly finishes his training. We hope he'll be in place by the end of the year.

- The Minneapolis area is being covered for two months by Brad Shipley on loan from Montana. Thanks to Larry James and Mike Gentry for this loan to help us keep up with our present workloads.

Thanks also to Rich David for keeping our customers in two areas happy. I'll be calling on all of you to help as the need arises. Please let me know with as much lead time as you can when you'll be able to help.

NEW AREA/ OPPORTUNITY

A new area is being opened in Walker. It is for 40 percent travel, and the sales rep will have to build up the area as well as pick up overloads in other areas.

NEXT MEETING

6/18/__. E-mail/call me by 6/10/__ with topics/issues you'd like included on the agenda.

Memo #6 First Draft

TUITION REIMBURSEMENT PLAN

Through the Tuition Plan employees have the opportunity to participate in academic programs in order to pursue personal and career interests, further their formal education, and increase their job-related expertise.

Encourage employees when they approach you, as supervisors, for information and advice.

Encourage them to participate. As long as courses are academic and do not interfere with the normal work schedule, employees may enroll. Advise them to submit a completed application early enough for approval. Applications (Form 4732) are available to you to give to them from the Office of the Director of Human Resources.

Remind employees to keep receipts. They'll need these in order to receive reimbursement.

Screen the applications carefully. If a course request doesn't seem in keeping with the intention of the plan, notify the employee and counsel her/him about what alternatives may exist. Otherwise, if approved, sign the application and forward it to the Human Resources Department. The Human Resources Department will notify the employee whether the application has been approved.

Tell the employee to submit proof of payment when the course is over, including receipts of all eligible expenses and proof of grade or successful completion, to the Human Resources Department. Then inform the employee that the Human Resources Department will forward a voucher to the cashier's office and a check will be issued within ten days.

Memo #6 Revision

TO:	All Supervisors
FROM:	Human Resources Department
RE:	How to Handle the Tuition Reimbursement Plan

VALUE OF PLAN

Through the Tuition Plan our employees have the opportunity to participate in academic programs in order to
- pursue personal and career interests
- further their formal education and
- increase their job-related expertise.

When an employee approaches you for information and advice about the plan, here's how to proceed.

PROCEDURE

Step	Action	
1	Encourage employees to participate as long as courses are academic and do not interfere with the normal work schedule.	
2	Obtain application (Form 4732) for employees from the Human Resources Department.	
3	Advise employees to submit the completed application form to you early enough for approval.	

IMPORTANT: Remind them to keep receipts. They'll need these in order to receive reimbursement.

Step	Action	
4	Screen applications carefully.	
5	If a course request is . . .	Then . . .
	not in keeping with the intention of the plan,	notify the employee and counsel her/him about alternatives.
	in keeping with the intention of the plan,	sign it and follow the next steps.
6	Forward it to the Director of Human Resources.	
7	Inform employee that Human Resources Department will inform her/him whether application has received final approval.	
8	Tell employee on successful completion of course to submit proof of payment, including receipts of eligible expenses and proof of grade or successful completion to Human Resources Department.	
9	Inform employee that Human Resources Department will forward this documentation to cashier's office, which will issue a check within ten days.	

Memo #7 First Draft

FROM:	
TO:	
CC:	
BCC:	
SUBJECT:	Conference Room

This is to ask you to reserve a conference room for the week starting Monday, 10 January. The conference room will be used for a series of seminars which are organized by the northern region and are scheduled to continue for whole week starting by 9:00 AM every day.

Since we are expecting a large audience to attend in most or special sessions of these seminars I would like you to reserve a conference room to accommodate about 50–75 people. Most of the speakers in these seminars are going to present their talks by using view graphs or slides. So, a view graph and a slide projector are needed to be set for this meeting room. I also need a long table to be set inside and next to the conference room entrance for those speakers who would like to leave material for distribution. Further, you should arrange for refreshments such as coffee/tea, fruit, and some cookies for the seminar hours.

Please reserve a conference room for us which provides above conditions and be sure to arrange projectors, a table and refreshments for whole week. All expenses for these seminars should be charged to us, account number 11111-000. I would appreciate if you could contact me as soon as you have arranged everything, and if you have any more questions please call me at the above extension. Thank you in advance for your cooperation.

Memo #7 Revision

FROM:	
TO:	
CC:	
BCC:	
SUBJECT:	Reserving Conference Room

Please reserve a conference room for the week starting Monday, 10 January. The conference room will be used for a series of seminars organized by the northern region and scheduled for the whole week. Here are the details.

TIME:
9:00 AM- 4:30 PM

ROOM SIZE/SET UP:
Accommodate 50-75 people, chevron style with additional side table for handouts

EQUIPMENT/SET UP:
*   2 flip charts, one on each side of the room
*   2 overhead projectors, in front, on tables
*   LCD display, should presenters need it for computer-generated overheads
*   Tent cards and marking pens at each seat

REFRESHMENTS:
*   AM - coffee, bagels, fruit
*   PM - soft drinks, fruit and popcorn

BILLING:
Dept/Accnt #7777

CONTACT TO CONFIRM:
Dee Tayles, X799

Thanks!

CHUNKING EXERCISES

In the following exercise, try chunking. Though Jim Blaine gives the impression that he has chunked, he has not chunked sufficiently. He is reporting on more than just "sales" and "miscellaneous." And while you're creating new chunks, rewrite them as would a journalist—with eye-catching headlines.

Memo #8 First Draft

N.O. SALES COMPANY, INC.   **Needyville, Ohio 00000**

To: B. A. Critic   Date: March 16
From: Jim Blaine
Re: Field Report—February

The following is a Field Report for February for the division.

Sales

We are extremely pleased with our efforts in February, particularly with key products—Rho-Gam, Novasera, and Gravindex. Also, our cell-washing sales for February were extraordinarily excellent. We are pleased with sales and optimistic about our forecast attainment.

Miscellaneous

I, as well as other members of my division and many customers, have been complaining again about back-order problems.

A number of comments by customers indicate some need for corrections on our ACT-Hematology line. However, we also did $122,000 worth of sales of that line this month, so, hopefully, the problems are not major. However, if they are, we may have repercussions. We have added new products to our ACT-Hematology line and we continue to have problems with the competition. Additionally, we placed a price increase on our entire product line.

During February, Thom Kish resigned. He accepted a sales position with Beta Labs. His reason for leaving was compensation. We will begin checking the background experience of candidates to fill the position immediately.

Major competition during February remains the Beta Labs.

This concludes my Field Report for February. If you have any questions relative to the above, please feel free to call.

Here's a chunked version to compare with yours.

Memo #8 Revision

TO: B. A. Critic   Date: March 16

FROM: Jim Blaine

RE: Field Report—February

February sales in the division were strong. We have introduced new products and considered changing old ones. Problems with our competitors, our order department, and our compensation plan remain.

SALES: Strong to Excellent	February sales of our key products—Rho-Gam, Novasera, and Gravindex 90—rose by 8.9 percent over last year. Cell-washing sales were especially strong, posting a 13.6 percent gain. We should have no trouble meeting the forecast.
	Beta Labs remains our major competitor.
ACT-HEMATOLOGY LINE: Old and New Products and Problems	Our customers have suggested changes in this line. Sales remain robust—$122,000 in February—so such changes are not urgent. Because we want to maintain strong sales, however, we're carefully reviewing these suggestions.
	We've continued to add new products to this line. The recent across-the-line price hike, however, is likely to increase the heat from our competitors, who are capturing larger market shares each month.
BACK ORDERS: No Remedy in Sight?	Customers continue to complain about back orders—with reason. Is the automation of our inventory proceeding on schedule?
PERSONNEL: Where Competition Hurts	Thom Kish resigned to accept a sales position at Beta Labs. His sole reason for leaving us was our compensation and benefits package, which is not keeping pace with the industry standard.
	We hope to fill his position soon.

ANOTHER CHUNKING EXERCISE

Help! Now chunk this overly detailed monthly report. All you need to do is label each paragraph!

Memo #9 First Draft

TO: VP Sales
FROM: Seymour Sales, Regional Manager
SUBJECT: August Monthly Recap – Region W

During the month of August there were two new accounts opened in the region. One, called Karmine's, is an upscale Italian restaurant with our Best Beer, Fizzy Pop, and Cool Spring beverages. The owners of Karmine's are still discussing the possibility of our draught wine. The other new account is a coffee-shop type restaurant called Marty's. We are exclusive in this account with Best Beer, Fizzy Pop, and Cool Spring beverages.

Sales for Region W are consistent at a 1.6% increase year-to-date versus 3% for company. Route X performed best, with year-to-date sales up 3.4% for Best Beer, 21% for Fizzy Pop, .7% for Cool Spring, 2.9% for Cool Spring Carbonated, and a total of 3.4%. Route Y continues as the only route to show declines, with year-to-date sales of -2.4% for Best Beer, 19.8% for Fizzy Pop, -1.2% for Cool Spring, -8.5% for Cool Spring Carbonated and a total of -1.2%.

I feel the demography in Route Z best indicates why sales have declined. As in our other high-income areas the market-share surveys consistently show the relative strength of competing brands. This fact coupled with the aggressive price promoting of our competitors partially explains the problems on this sales route. The sales rep on Route Z has done an exceptional job of selling promotional displays and reduced price. Due to the competition's more generous price reductions and extended post-off periods, they have succeeded in being more visible in the past years. I feel that, as difficult as it is to measure, The Price Club's tremendous volume and proximity to Route Z has had its effect on the route's volume.

One outstanding accomplishment for the region was that three out of four sales reps had the three best records for special deliveries companywide.

Moving on to out-of-code product for the month, Region W did not perform as well as in the past months. The great deal of product that expired during the period with the region's emphasis on getting it out of the trade contributed to higher-than-average totals. Route Z had an unacceptable amount of out-of-code due to negligence on the sales rep's behalf but this sales rep realizes the severity of the problem and will correct it.

Region W continues to show strong results in most categories. In my upcoming fourth-quarter action plan, steps will be taken to reverse the few negative trends mentioned here as well as capitalize on the momentum of those areas with positive trends.

Here's a revised, chunked version to compare with yours.

Memo #9 Revision

TO: VP Sales
FROM: Seymour Sales, Regional Manager
SUBJECT: August Monthly Recap – Region W

Region W continues to show strong results in sales and new accounts. Declining sales on Route Z and high volume of out-of-code performance were problems this month. We've initiated a plan to reverse these few negative trends and improve our otherwise solid record.

SALES REPS' STERLING RECORDS	Of the four Region W sales reps, three had the best records, companywide, for special deliveries.
TWO NEW ACCOUNTS	• Karmine's, an upscale Italian restaurant, now carries our Best Beer draught, Fizzy Pop, and Cool Spring beverages. The owners are discussing the possibility of draught wine. • Marty's, a coffee shop, exclusively carries our Best Beer, Fizzy Pop, and Cool Spring beverages.

MIXED SALES TRENDS FOR REGION W

Sales are consistent at a 1.6% increase year-to-date versus 3% for company. Route X was our best performer in year-to-date sales. Route Y continues to show declines.

	Route X	Route Y
Best Beer	+3.4%	-2.4%
Fizzy Pop	+21%	+19.8%
Cool Spring	+.7%	-1.2%
Cool Spring Carbonated	+2.9%	-8.5%
Overall sales	+3.4%	-1.2%

REASONS FOR DECLINING SALES ON ROUTE Z

Continued declining sales can be explained by these factors:

• the strength of competing brands in high-income areas
• competitors' aggressive price promoting and extended post-off periods
• The Price Club's tremendous volume and proximity to Route Z

UNUSUAL OUT-OF-CODE PERFORMANCE

Region W did not perform as well this month as in the past because

• moving a great deal of our product out of the trade contributed to higher-than-average totals;
• Route Z sales underperformed.

STEPS TAKEN

My 4Q Action Plan outlines what we've done—and will do—to reverse our trends and build momentum.

USE TABLES, GRAPHS, AND OTHER VISUALS TO GIVE THE BIG PICTURE FAST

Though language is our primary communications channel, it has shortcomings. Complex, detailed information is often better presented in a nonprose format. When you want your reader to get the big picture fast, a visual, rather than words, will create the impression readily. With computer graphics accessible, it is no longer as time-consuming to create valuable visuals as it once was.

Use a table . . . when your reader needs to have exact figures or information easily available and wants to pick out quickly a particular figure from the group.

Shipping Selection Guide		
	Under 1000 Miles	**Over 1000 Miles**
Time urgent	Overnight Air	Overnight Air
Time urgent/cost limited	2nd Day Air	Priority Mail
Only cost limited	Pony Express	Sav-U Trucking
No rush	Parcel Post	Stagecoach

Use a graph . . . when your reader needs to grasp trends, proportions, or comparisons quickly.

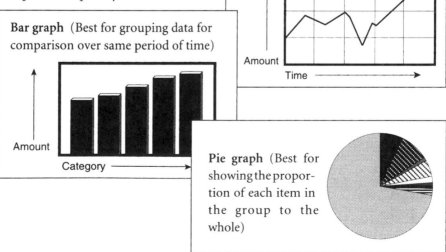

Broken-line graph (Best for showing progress over time)

Amount

Time

Bar graph (Best for grouping data for comparison over same period of time)

Amount

Category

Pie graph (Best for showing the proportion of each item in the group to the whole)

Use a pictograph . . . when your reader may not understand written instructions.

Use a flow chart . . . when your reader needs to understand the steps of a process.

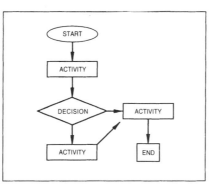

Use an illustration cut-away, or photograph . . . when your reader needs to grasp/see details of an object. Label the parts.

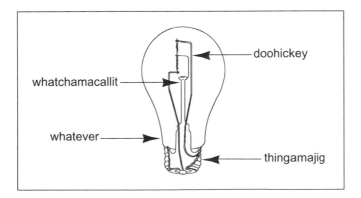

USE POWERPOINT® SLIDES TO AID YOUR ORAL PRESENTATIONS

Microsoft's PowerPoint program can help you generate slides that put pizzazz into your oral presentations and help you prepare appealing training manuals. Combine words with graphics to ensure your reader will not only "get" your message quickly, but will also remember it long after your presentation.

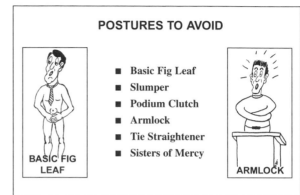

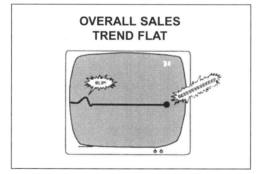

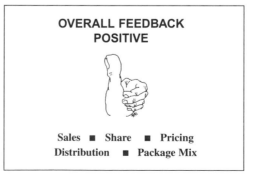

A PowerPoint slide needn't be a page full of text. If it's intended to be a visual aid to your presentation, ask yourself, "What does my visual show?" not "What does my visual say?"

These guidelines help ensure powerful slide presentations.

- Remember the 6x6 rule (no more than six words across or six lines down).

- Use a large enough font (18 point minimum, 24 to 48 point for headings).

- Use key words, <u>not</u> full sentences.

- Accent with color, combination of upper and lower case letters, and graphics.

Turn this . . .

into . . .

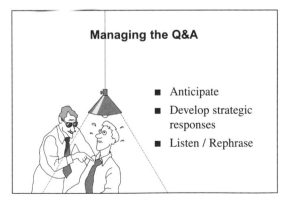

TYING IT TOGETHER WITH TRANSITIONS

Transitions glue your paragraphs and sentences together smoothly. They help maintain the logic of your writing. In fact, they often help the logic stand out more clearly. Use linking expressions to bridge the gaps between points.

Transitions ⮕

To indicate another point	After that	Finally	Second
	Also	First	Then
	Another	Furthermore	To begin with
	At last	In addition	Too
	At the outset	In conclusion	To sum up
	Besides	Moreover	
To indicate another time, place, or sequence	Above all	Further	Soon
	After all	In summary	Still
	Again	Later	Then
	At length	Meanwhile	Too
	Finally	Next	
	First	Not long after	
To indicate results	As a result	Hence	Thus
	Consequently	Therefore	
To show contrast/ exception to what has been said	But conversely	Nevertheless	
	Even though	On the contrary	
	However	On the other hand	
	In spite of	Otherwise	
	Instead		
To show relationships	Accordingly	Similarly	
	Likewise	Such	
To introduce examples	An example of this	For instance	That is
	For example	Namely	
		Such as	

SUMMARY OF TECHNIQUES THAT SHOWCASE YOUR IDEAS AND REVEAL YOUR KNACK FOR ORGANIZING

Writing well includes formatting information so it is readable, remember-able, and easily retrievable. In addition to bottom-lining, headlining, chunk-ing, and graphing, you can draw from a variety of mainstay techniques listed here to showcase your ideas and organization.

To reveal important points, use

- Boldface
- Bottom-lining
    - Abstract
    - Introductory summary
    - Executive summary
- Bullets (*parallel structure, please*)
- Capital letters/Attractive typography
- Forecast statements
    - Subject lines
    - Headlines
    - Subheadings
- Indentations/White space
- Numbering (*parallel structure, please*)
- Transitional words/phrases
- Underlining
- Visuals
    - Tables
    - Graphs
    - Pictographs
    - Charts
    - Illustrations/Photographs

When you have finished your draft, ask yourself these questions. Your answers will help you order, arrange, and present your content.

1. How does my reader want to use this information?

2. What order/arrangement will make the information easier to use?

3. Will that order help effectively communicate the message?

4. What arrangement will help get the results I want?

5. What is the best logical and/or psychological order (order of importance, size, time sequence, other)?

6. Can some information be understood more easily in a graph, chart, table?

7. Will boldface, lists, or headlines help clarify my information?

8. Does any information bear repeating?

9. Are there natural transitions between my paragraphs and/or points?

10. Is the copy visually appealing (broken up by tables, graphics, relatively short paragraphs, white space, indentations, etc.)?

8

Structuring Your Sentences—
to Clarify Your Intent and Add Style

We started the process of improving your writing through first thinking about the big picture—the bottom line. Then we worked on chunking your paragraphs and visually supporting your message on the page. Now let's think about the smaller units in your writing—your sentences (and later, your words)—and how they can clarify your message as well as display your own style.

One of the richest means for expressing your style is the arrangement of words in a sentence—your sentence structure. Let me jog your seventh-grade grammar memories with the four kinds of sentences: simple (one main thought); compound (two main thoughts); complex (one main and one subordinate thought); and compound-complex (two or more complex structures). Compound, complex, and compound-complex sentences have quite precise relationships between the clauses they contain. Keep in mind that a clause is made up of a group of words containing a subject and its verb. Main clauses, called independent clauses, are thoughts that can stand by themselves as complete sentences. Subordinate clauses, called dependent clauses, are thoughts that cannot stand alone but need the main clause to make sense.

Simple:	Steve's promotion appeared in the *Wall Street Journal.*
Compound:	Steve's promotion appeared in the *Wall Street Journal*, but the writer omitted a key point.
Complex:	Steve's promotion appeared in the *Wall Street Journal*, though the writer omitted a key point.
Compound-Complex:	Steve's promotion appeared in the *Wall Street Journal*, though the writer omitted a key point, and his company's stock rose the same day, surprising the analysts.

Experiment to develop sentences that accurately capture your intent. Revise. Vary your word order, your sentence length, the type of sentence. Shift a key word or phrase to the beginning, to the end. Discover what best accomplishes your purpose *and* suits your taste. Writing that sounds like you will appeal more to your reader, but only by experimenting will you discover your own true style and "voice."

While most business readers prefer the basic, subject-verb-object structure, variety is the key to holding interest. Toward that end, what follows are suggestions for coordinating, emphasizing, and de-emphasizing information through sentence structure.

COMBINE SENTENCES TO CREATE EMPHASIS AND ELIMINATE WORDINESS

Here's a paragraph that needs its sentences combined so it reads more smoothly. You'll note the majority of sentences are simple ones, and the effect of several such sentences in a row is to make the writer sound linguistically naive—in other words, dull.

Example #1

We need to evaluate our competitive position. We need to know what effect the marketing of import beers has on the Best Brands market. Import beers have been increasing in sales for years. This has happened as the number of ethnic restaurants has increased. There has recently been an increase of these beers elsewhere. Mexican, Canadian, and German beers are available in supermarkets. They are available through other nonethnic distribution channels. Strategies must be developed. They must be developed to maintain Best Brands' share in the distribution network. They must be developed to increase market share. We need to respond. We need to respond to the change in the composition of the beer market.

By combining some of the short sentences—leaving out words, adding transition words, or changing word endings—you create a more sophisticated sound. Have a look.

Example #1 Revision

We need to ~~evaluate our competitive position. We need to~~ know
have
what effect ~~the marketing of~~ import beers ~~has~~ on the Best Brands
It's clear that   sales
market. ^Import beers^ have been increasing ~~in sales for years. This~~

~~has happened~~ as the number of ethnic restaurants has increased. ~~There~~
And
~~has recently been an increase of these beers elsewhere.~~ ^Mexican,
now   as well as
Canadian, and German beers are ^available in supermarkets. ~~They are~~
Consequently, if we develop sound
~~available~~ through other nonethnic distribution channels. ^ *S*trategies
to increase market share,   we'll
^~~must be developed. They must be developed to~~ maintain Best

Brands' share in the distribution network. ~~They must be developed~~ to
Clearly
increase market share. ~~We need to respond.~~ ^ We need to respond to

the change in the composition of the beer market.

While sentence combining helps you get rid of repetition and choppiness, it also permits you to vary the rhythm of your writing. That variety gives your writing a touch of class. You come across as polished, powerful, and decisive—without sounding pretentious.

COMBINE SENTENCES TO PRESENT IDEAS OF PARALLEL IMPORTANCE ⁻

Some sentences or thoughts you will combine are equal in importance. Though you may wish to show the relationship between or among them, you may not want to designate one as more significant or influential than another. Compound sentences exist so we can express ideas of like importance in relation to each another. And we can indicate those relationships by using the words on these lists to connect ideas of equal value.

Coordinating Conjunctions	*Conjunctive Adverbs*
, and	; consequently,
, but	; furthermore,
, nor	; hence,
, or	; however,
, so	; moreover,
, yet	; nevertheless,
	; otherwise,
	; subsequently,
	; therefore,
	; thus,

Combine these sentences, linking them with one of the words above. You'll find many combinations possible.

Before: The differences between the two health-care plans are significant. We should provide the staff with a choice between them.

Rewrite:

Before: Community involvement has always been encouraged by management. A local environmental group has asked us to join their cause.

Rewrite:

FOCUS ON EMPHASIS

Combine each pair of sentences into one new sentence that emphasizes one part of the information and de-emphasizes the other. Use one of these words to introduce one of your ideas.

Subordinating Conjunctions			*Relative Pronouns*
after	before	unless	that
although	if	until	which
as	provided	when	who
as if	since	whenever	whom
as long as	so that	where	whose
as soon as	then	wherever	
because	though	whether	
		while	

For instance,

Before: The computer is obsolete. It is using valuable storage space.

Rewrite: The computer, which is obsolete, is using valuable storage space.

1. **Before:** Ken Cramer has become a division representative in Michigan. He graduated from the University of Indiana last month.

   Rewrite:

2. **Before:** Their consumer-awareness program came into existence recently. Ours has been implemented for six years.

   Rewrite:

3. **Before:** The forklift was no longer working. It was auctioned to the highest bidder.

   Rewrite:

4. **Before:** His ad brought 300 letters from people who wanted the job. The letters were from highly experienced people.

   Rewrite:

(See page 75 for possible rewrites to compare with yours.)

FOCUS ON ELIMINATING WORDINESS

Combine each pair of sentences into one by changing the information in one sentence to a modifying phrase or word.

For example,

Before: Next Generation now employs 1500 people. It was founded ten years ago.

Rewrite: Founded ten years ago, Next Generation now employs 1500 people.

1. **Before:** Paul Bern is a sales rep in the state of Maine. He spoke at the Kiwanis Club last week.

   Rewrite:

2. **Before:** Her company's leave policy is less desirable. Her leave policy doesn't provide the same range of options as ours.

   Rewrite:

3. **Before:** The Target-Market Program would involve a student, quite possibly a senior, working a specific number of hours per week for one semester. A semester would be approximately fourteen weeks.

   Rewrite:

4. **Before:** On January 21, Debra Maurer joined our group as an intern. Debra is a senior at Rutgers University, majoring in business.

   Rewrite:

5. **Before:** The copier is no longer working. We gave it away.

   Rewrite:

(See page 75 for possible rewrites to compare with yours.)

From page 73— **Possible Rewrites to Compare with Yours.**

1. Ken Cramer, who graduated from the University of Indiana last month, has become a division representative in Michigan.

2. While their consumer-awareness program came into existence recently, ours has been implemented for six years.

3. Because the forklift was no longer working, it was auctioned to the highest bidder.

4. His ad brought 300 letters from people who were highly experienced and who wanted the job.

From page 74— **Possible Rewrites to Compare with Yours.**

1. Paul Bern, a sales rep in Maine, spoke at the Kiwanis Club last week.

2. Her company's leave policy, lacking the same options as ours, is less desirable.

3. The Target-Market Program would involve a student, quite possibly a senior, working a specific number of hours per week for one fourteen-week semester.

4. On January 21, Debra Maurer, a senior majoring in business at Rutgers University, joined our group as an intern.

5. We gave the broken copier away.

VARY SENTENCE LENGTH TO CREATE RHYTHM

Writers who are alert to sentence structure are also writers who've got rhythm. Pleasingly varied rhythm is the reward of experimenting with sentence length and structure. Poor rhythm is the penalty paid by the unadventurous.

For example, here's poor rhythm due to the sameness of sentence structure and sentence length:

> The warehouse was scrubbed from floor to ceiling, and the trucks were newly painted. The warehouse supervisor greeted us at the entrance, and our review started at eight o'clock. The division manager was well satisfied, and the principal was noticeably relieved.

And here is its pleasing revision:

> At eight o'clock, our review began. The warehouse supervisor greeted us at the entrance to the warehouse, which had been scrubbed from floor to ceiling. Even the trucks were newly painted. When the division manager expressed his satisfaction, the principal looked relieved.

Varying Rhythm with Sentence Length

Number of words per sentence	
10	Successful writing usually averages fifteen-to-twenty words per sentence. But that doesn't mean you need to write all your sentences to conform to these limits, because you would surely bore most of
29, 3	your readers with your never-changing pace. Instead, vary lengths. Your readers will enjoy the shifting rhythm and, in fact, will find
22	themselves caught up in your effective control of sentence length.
4	Short sentences provide emphasis! The shorter the sentence the
8, 5	bigger its punch. Short sentences move your writing. But too many
9	short ones, huddled together, don't work. Rather, they make your
8, 3	writing choppy or singsongy. Or juvenile sounding. Try plopping a short sentence or two in between your longer ones, and marvel at the
24	resulting power it will give to your writing.
	Longer sentences slow down the pace and can help balance your
12	writing. Like a river or a road, long sentences wind their way along a stretch of paper, more relaxed and quiet than short sentences, deliberate and slow, as they unfold and describe, releasing information little by little, providing details almost endlessly until they decide
46	finally to stop. Although such sentences are occasionally useful—to change the pace—they subordinate, or bury, too much information in them and, as a result, are generally ineffective for presenting your
33	major message or idea.
2	The answer? It's the combination of long and short, mixed wisely,
19	that makes your audience say, "That was a good memo."

(14.8 words—Average sentence length [ASL] in this selection.)

| 10 | 29 | 3 | 22 | 4 | 8 | 5 | 9 | 8 | 3 | 24 | 12 | 46 | 33 | 2 | 19 |

EIGHT WAYS TO ADD EMPHASIS AND ELEGANCE TO SENTENCES

THE HEAD-ON SENTENCE

The head-on sentence is structured so that its main point appears first, followed by other phrases or clauses that expand or support it. This is the structure preferred by business readers because it is straightforward. But putting *all* sentences in such a format isn't good business sense.

Example: <u>The solution must be finely honed,</u> lest our marketing strategists err too much on the side of pricing, only to find that we can lose market share by, more simply, mere lack of coverage.

Example: <u>Ed Doherty is the best candidate</u> for the job, having earned the respect of his colleagues on many difficult assignments and having worked for seven years for a major architectural firm.

Example: <u>Lisa's recommendation received quick approval</u> because it was well thought out and presented in a friendly tone so that no one walked away slighted or offended by her comments.

THE BUILD-UP SENTENCE

The build-up sentence is structured so that its main idea is suspended until the very end, thereby drawing your reader's eye and mind along to an emphatic conclusion. This type of sentence is also known as the periodic sentence.

Example: While the division managers encourage personnel to experiment on their own initiative with new and different marketing strategies, <u>these managers cannot—and will not— justify unprofessional practices.</u>

Example: In restaurants, especially on draught, and even more than the imports, <u>Best Beer is a dominant factor.</u>

Example: Satisfied that the business proposition is sound and that the implementation costs and sales estimates provided are appropriately conservative, <u>I support your plan.</u>

Example: In their small, homemade basement still, where the only thing brewing was problems, <u>the product was more ail than ale.</u>

Example: Having conducted extensive market research, saved his seed money, and summoned his courage, <u>he opened the doors of his new business in February.</u>

The Rhetorical Question

Another sentence that helps to focus your reader's attention on a problem or issue is the rhetorical question—a question that requires no specific response from your reader but often helps introduce your own views as the writer. In some cases a rhetorical question may serve as a topic sentence in a paragraph; in other cases a series of rhetorical questions may spotlight key issues you want your reader to consider.

> **Example:** Why all the mystery about what prizes we'll be offering as incentives for the next sales promotion? It has everything to do with our not yet knowing their availability and nothing to do with keeping you uninformed.
>
> **Example:** Will we increase our market share? Will we be the leader in the industry? When will it all happen?
>
> **Example:** Who knows what evil lurks within the hearts of men? The Shadow knows.

The Reversed Sentence

A reversal of customary or expected sentence order is yet another effective stylistic strategy. Reversal injects freshness, unexpectedness, and originality into your writing.

> **Example:** He is a lost man. *(customary order)*
> He is a man lost. *(reversed order)*
>
> **Example:** I find that these conditions are indisputable: the economy has taken a drastic downturn, costs have soared, and jobs are at a premium. *(customary order)*
> That the economy has taken a drastic downturn; that costs have soared; that jobs are at a premium— these are the conditions that I find indisputable. *(reversed order)*
>
> **Example:** The question is: to be or not to be. *(customary order)*
> To be or not to be: That is the question. *(reversed order)*
>
> **Example:** Try, try again, if at first you don't succeed. *(customary order)*
> If at first you don't succeed, try, try again. *(reversed order)*
>
> **Example:** He is not a fine candidate. *(customary order)*
> He is a fine candidate. Not! *(reversed order)*

THE INTERRUPTED SENTENCE

Interrupting the normal flow of a sentence by inserting comments is a strategy you may use to call attention to your aside, to emphasize a word or phrase, to render a special effect (such as forcefulness), or to make your style a little more informal. Use these carefully, since too many insertions may distract your reader and disrupt your train of thought.

Example: You will be receiving shortly, if you haven't already, the new guidelines for the online training program. *(an aside)*

Example: The evidence, if reliable, could send the VP of Finance to prison. *(an aside)*

Example: These companies—ours as well as theirs—must show more profits. *(emphasis)*

Example: This, supervisors, is the prime reason for your cost overruns. *(forcefulness)*

Example: Jeans (as long as they're not the ripped variety) are fine for Friday's casual-dress day at the office. *(clarification)*

THE COORDINATED/SUBORDINATED SENTENCE

You can coordinate ideas or subordinate some to others, or use a mixture of both to create different stylistic effects.

Coordinating promotes ideas to equal standing; subordinating tends to tighten your writing and focus your reader's attention on your main clause. Here are examples of these two strategies:

Example: During the balance of this year, the company expects to issue $100,000,000 of long-term debt and equity securities and may guarantee up to $200,000,000 of new corporate bonds. *(coordinating)*

Example: Although the company expects to issue $100,000,000 of long-term debt and equity securities during the balance of this year, it may also guarantee up to $200,000,000 of new corporate bonds. *(subordinating)*

THE PARALLEL SENTENCE

A parallel sentence is one in which adjacent phrases and clauses are constructed in a similar fashion. The result is a balanced sentence, with an even, rhythmic flow of thoughts.

Generally, three items in a series provide a natural rhythm. Remember

- Churchill's "blood, sweat, and tears"
- faith, hope, and charity
- Lincoln's "government of the people, by the people, and for the people"

Example: These ecological problems are of concern to scientists, to government officials, and to our company.

Example: Our attorneys have argued that the trademark is ours, that our rights have been violated, and that appropriate compensation is required.

Example: What interested me was the contrast between the rich and the poor, the strong and the weak, the wise and the foolish.

Example: "I came; I saw; I conquered."—*Julius Caesar*

Example: He was respected not only for his intelligence, but also for his integrity.

Example: "To err is human; to forgive, divine."—*Alexander Pope*

Example: "Ask not what your country can do for you—ask what you can do for your country."—*John F. Kennedy*

THE MINOR SENTENCE

Otherwise known as a fragment, the incomplete, or minor, sentence serves often in advertising and *can* work, if used sparingly and knowingly, in your memos.

Example: Do we intend to pull the product off the shelves? Not on your life.

Example: When?

Example: Whatever.

Example: We sent our answer to the competition. No more shenanigans!

Example: What would she give for a few more employees like Susan? The world.

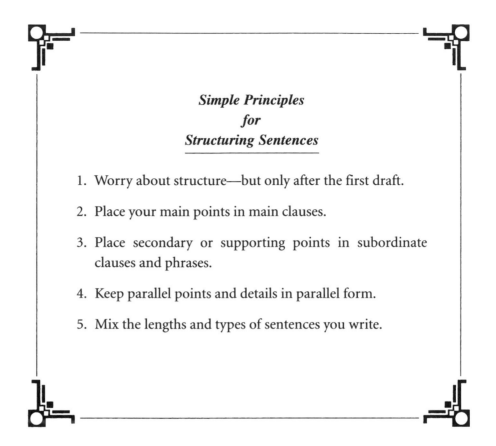

Simple Principles
for
Structuring Sentences

1. Worry about structure—but only after the first draft.

2. Place your main points in main clauses.

3. Place secondary or supporting points in subordinate clauses and phrases.

4. Keep parallel points and details in parallel form.

5. Mix the lengths and types of sentences you write.

Part 4 Choosing Your Words Wisely for Conciseness and Consideration

If I had more time, I would write a shorter letter.
                                                    Blaise Pascal

"Basically to be, or,
on the other hand, not to be,
that, undoubtedly, is actually
the vital question one has
to consider for certain."

9
Getting Rid of Sentence Clutter

In previous chapters we've looked at the macro issues tied to your business writing: stating the big picture, bottom-lining your message, structuring paragraphs and sentences to support and showcase your message. In this chapter we look at the micro issues: individual words and phrases and how each word helps—or hinders—getting your message across.

Remember school?

> "Now, class, for your assignment, I want you to write an essay in which you discuss Macbeth's tragic flaw. Be sure to cite adequate proof from the play and spell and punctuate correctly. And remember, you must turn in at least five hundred words."

Sound familiar? Chances are it was an all-too-familiar assignment from well-intentioned though misguided teachers in our past. Such assignments—emphasizing and rewarding quantity—partially account for why today's business writing contains so much clutter. We added filler to satisfy the teacher's minimum-word-count requirement.

A second reason for the deadwood that floats in (and bloats) our memos and reports: believing that to impress requires fifty-cent words and phrases; that stating something simply will not sound good enough. (Those who let this notion reign need to be reminded of Mark Twain. "Why," said he, "should I say *metropolis* when they pay me the same for *city*?")

And a third reason why much business correspondence is flabby? Simply not knowing how to find and then eliminate the fat.

I'll remedy that by showing you ten forms of flab. If you follow the suggestions here, you'll be able to trim the unwanted pounds from your writing.

CUTTING OUT TEN FORMS OF CLUTTER

Omit each and every single word for which you do not have a use.

or

Omit useless words.

Ready?

1. ELIMINATE HEAVY SENTENCE STARTERS

Much of the clutter in writing "hangs" in the front of sentences, making them top-heavy. When you draft, top-heavy sentences

> *"If in doubt, throw it out."*

are a natural phenomenon. Because getting started is hard, you often struggle or stutter over those first few words. No wonder you fall back on phrases well within your grasp whenever you begin to write. And, as each successive sentence is a new start, those ready-made phrases flood your writing.

While they are helpful in getting you through your first drafts, these wordy constructions are not needed in your final copy. Watch for and eliminate "It Ache," "I Ache," "There Ache," and "Here Ache."

"It ache"

"It ache" is the unnecessary use or overuse of an anticipatory construction at the start of a sentence. A leading symptom of clutter, it's easy to find—and eliminate—since the real message of the sentence follows the anticipatory construction. Just drop the "it" clause from the sentence and begin instead with the message.

See how unnecessary the "it" construction is in the following examples.

"It Ache"

- ~~It should be noted that~~ my budget of $900,000 for next year is a 22 percent decrease from . . .
- ~~It would be helpful to~~ view the annual organizational-planning audit as an ongoing . . .
- ~~It is hoped that~~ this assignment can be completed within three months . . .
- ~~It is understood~~ during the period of convalescence the employee will. . . .
- ~~It is concluded that~~ improvements in assembly reliability may be made by using smaller, higher-density SMA packages, extended pad metallization, and shaped joints.
- ~~It was found that~~ the observed thermocyclic-fatigue life of the most vulnerable joints is lower than one might predict.

A few more "it aches" worth avoiding:

- It is worthy of note . . .

- It is important to consider/note . . .

- It must be remembered that . . .

- It is imperative that . . .

- It has come to my attention that . . .

"I Ache"

> *Do you wish people to think well of you? Don't speak well of yourself!*
>
> Blaise Pascal

"I ache" is the unnecessary use of *I* in writing. It is one of several sentence starters cluttering your writing. Worse, however, is that it also focuses the writing on you, the writer, rather than on your reader. Such a construction makes the writer the omnipotent one in a sentence—or a memo. Through too many *I*'s, see how important the writer has made himself in the following letter. "Ay, Ay, Ay!"

Memo #1

FROM:	E. Gotist
TO:	U.R. Second
CC:	
BCC:	
SUBJECT:	Project

I would like to start a new project. I need your blessing. I would like to do the following. I want to make a list of all accounts that are not active and delete them as well as their network drives. I also want to check the last time some of these people logged in. I have seen some users with accounts still active but they have not used them since February. I plan to make a spreadsheet with the status of all logins that are in question. I could reclaim space back on our servers and clean all up. I hope you will say yes.

Many writers make the opposite mistake—of avoiding *I* at all costs. (That's why we choke reading about "the undersigned," "the writer," and that good ol' nebulous "we.") The answer lies in having the shy and the egotist alike use *I* deliberately, sparingly, and appropriately, to create the right effect—one that's not overbearing.

See what I mean in this revision.

Memo #1 Revision

From:	Notta E. Gotist
To:	U.R. Second
CC:	
BCC:	
Subject:	Request for Project Approval

Ron:

Your blessing for me to start a new project will let us reclaim much needed space on our server. If you agree, I can start right away to

- make a list of inactive accounts and delete them as well as their network drives;
- check the last login date of all "active" users (some listed as active have not logged on for six months); and
- create a spreadsheet with the status of all logins in question so we can verify active/inactive status.

Do I have a green light?

"There Ache" and "Here Ache"

Like their first cousin, "It Ache," "There Ache" and "Here Ache" are often unnecessary sentence starters.

- There are some circumstances that suggest . . .
- There were eight divisions that underwent audits.
- There is a tremendous amount of potential in the department, and most of it is, as yet, untapped.
- There are three people who can sign . . .
- In some divisions of the company there are special task forces being assigned to resolve that marketing problem.
- There are two options available to us to consider.

Other Sentence Starters

Here are additional sentence starters that may help you through the initial phase of getting words on paper. The solution to this form of clutter is easy: Note that the message follows the false sentence start, and simply remove the unnecessary windup and get right to the pitch.

- As per your memo/request/conversation . . .
- In reference to the above captioned subject . . .
- Attached please find . . .
- Enclosed please find . . .
- Please be advised . . .
- As you are aware. . .

Exercising "It Ache"

Now, streamline these by getting rid of the "it ache" in them.

1. It seems that of the two divisions, Sharon Doe's has greater sales.
   Revision: _____

2. It should be noted that the recommendations contained in this document are based on the results obtained from various focus groups.
   Revision: _____

3. It was found that there arc more than 29,000 customers in the file, while it is estimated that only half of those are still active customers.
   Revision: _____

4. It was the personnel manager who requested the policy be rewritten.
   Revision: _____

5. It is necessary to sign the documents by midnight, January 1.
   Revision: _____

Exercising the I

Revise, revise. In each case, the sentence is tighter without the *I*'s pulling attention back to the writer. Use *I*, but sparingly, so that when you do, it has power. It's better business to place yourself in the background and let the issue and the reader have center stage.

6. I thought you would like to know we have six out of seven people in Region V at over 100 percent of their service target.
   Revision: _____

7. I also notice that snack-size sales are starting to increase.
   Revision: _____

8. I would truly like to thank each of you for doing your part to make this happen.
   Revision: _____

9. I am of the opinion that this will . . .
   Revision: _____

10. I want to thank you for your decision to add to . . .
    Revision: _____

(continued)

See page 93 for suggested rewrites to these sentences.

Exercising the I (continued)

11. We feel our department is well qualified . . .
    Revision: _____

12. Let me preface my remarks by suggesting that there are no quick and easy ways . . .
    Revision: _____

Retiring Tired Sentence Starters

Remove these tired sentence starters from each sentence. Make each fresher, tighter, less trite sounding.

13. There is a growing sense of confidence within the various departments that we can be of help to them.
    Revision: _____

14. Last November there was a good response from the managers.
    Revision: _____

15. As per your request dated November 10, I am completing an action plan for the Iowa market by December 1.
    Revision: _____

16. Attached please find the monthly stats for each market.
    Revision: _____

17. Enclosed please find the responses from Regions I and III.
    Revision: _____

18. Please be advised that the new E-mail system will be online January 1.
    Revision: _____

19. In reference to the above-captioned subject, I have the following suggestions.
    Revision: _____

20. As you are aware, the competition will be introducing its new premium brand on March 15.
    Revision: _____

See page 93 for suggested rewrites to these sentences.

Suggested Rewrites to Sentences on Pages 91 and 92

1. Of the two divisions, Sharon Doe's has greater sales.

2. This report is based on focus group results.

3. Approximately half of the 29,000+ customers in the file are active.

4. The personnel manager requested the policy be rewritten.

5. Please sign the documents by midnight, January 1.

6. Six out of seven people in Region V are over 100 percent of their service target.

7. Snack-size sales are improving.

8. Thanks for doing your part to make this happen.

9. This will . . .

10. Thank you for your decision to add to . . .

11. Our department is well qualified . . .

12. No quick and easy ways exist to . . .

13. Confidence is growing within the various departments that we can help them.

14. Last November's response from managers was strong.

15. As requested, I'll complete an action plan for the Iowa market by December 1.

16. The attached monthly stats for each market indicate . . .

17. The enclosed responses from Regions I and III . . .

18. The new E-mail system will be online January 1.

19. I have the following suggestions for/about . . .

20. The competition will introduce its new premium brand on March 15.

2. ELIMINATE FLABBY SENTENCE MIDSECTIONS: "WHOERY," "WHICHERY," "THATERY"

"Whoery," "Whichery," and "Thatery" will lead you to flabby writing. But because these symptoms are easy to find in a sentence, they can be easily removed. They're forms of subclause-itis, and, like your appendix, aren't usually necessary. What's more, when they are pushed out of your sentence, one or two other lazy words from your sentence get pushed out with them as well.

"Whoery"

Wordy: John Sikorski is a manager who is held in high regard by the chairman of the board.

Revised: John Sikorski is a manager highly regarded by the chairman of the board.

Wordy: Jim King, who is our choice for the position, arrives Tuesday for his assessment.

Revised: Jim King, our choice for the position, arrives Tuesday for his assessment.

Wordy: Jan Diepe is the type of woman who always arrives on schedule.

Revised: Jan Diepe always arrives on schedule.

Wordy: Marta Patarca is an energetic administrative assistant who enjoys managing several tasks simultaneously.

Revised: Marta Patarca, an energetic admin, enjoys managing several tasks simultaneously.

"Whichery"

Wordy: Corum's, which is a subsidiary of Speedy, Inc., handles its own marketing and training.

Revised: Corum's, a Speedy, Inc. subsidiary, handles its own marketing and training.

Wordy: The $170.73 fee, which you paid in August, was the initial payment on the quarterly payment plan for your policy.

Revised: The $170.73 paid in August was the initial quarterly payment on your policy.

Wordy: The job, which April found highly agonizing, grew under the pressure of deadlines to be unbearable, and April quit.

Revised: This agonizing job grew unbearable under the pressure of deadlines, and April quit.

Wordy: An e-mail, which is an electronic piece of business writing less formal than a letter, serves to speed communication.

Revised: E-mail, less formal than a letter, speeds communication.

Wordy: In response to your recent letter concerning your policy, the following is a complete status for your reference, which does not include service charges.

Revised: Here's the status on your policy, excluding service charges.

"Thatery"

Wordy: All I can say is that he admitted to being late three times last week.

Revised: He admitted to being late three times last week.

Wordy: . . . develop a mission statement that is specific enough to be useful in providing clear direction for running the day-to-day business.

Revised: . . . develop a mission statement providing clear direction for running the day-to-day business.

Wordy: . . . agreed to write all advertising that will go into the program.

Revised: . . . agreed to write all program advertising.

"Exercisery"

Try trimming away the "whoery," "whichery," and "thatery."

1. Please remember that a key thing that will keep us number one and that you can personally help with is good service habits.
   Revision: _____

2. Review the points that are to be covered in each meeting.
   Revision: _____

3. She is a manager who rarely is seen, so her staff can do as they please.
   Revision: _____

4. The meeting, which is always too long and unfocused, is scheduled for next Tuesday.
   Revision: _____

5. The Fortune 500, which are usually considered blue-chip stocks, can be a roller coaster ride today.
   Revision: _____

Suggested Rewrites to Sentences

1. Good service habits will keep us number one. Please help.

2. Review the points to be covered in each meeting.

3. She is rarely seen, so her staff do as they please.

4. The meeting, always too long and unfocused, is scheduled for next Tuesday.

5. The Fortune 500, usually considered blue-chip stocks, can be a roller coaster ride today.

3. OMIT OVERLOADED NOUNS

Using nouns as adjectives and piling them up in front of one another is a proven way to clutter your sentences.

Example: Her job involves fault analysis systems troubleshooting manual preparation.

Hmm . . .   just what *is* her job? Or . . .

Our vehicle air conditioner compression cutoff device will reduce fuel consumption by 5 percent.

Or . . .   Global Positioning Interface Module Communications Processor Hardware Design Specification

Or . . .   You are invited to attend an introductory, self-paced, interactive, company-sponsored, interpersonal, team-oriented programming survey course.

Merely piling up too many adjectives in a row will at worst confound your reader; at best, slow the reader down. You may need to add a word or two to unclutter the ideas buried in a pile of nouns used as adjectives, but see what happens when you do. Here are the above examples, rewritten without over-loaded nouns:

Her job involves preparing manuals to help trouble-shoot fault-analysis systems.

Our compression cutoff device for vehicle air condition-ers will reduce fuel consumption by 5 percent.

And . . .   Global Positioning Interface Module: The Hardware Design Specification for the Communications Processor.

Last . . .   You are invited to a programming survey course that is
  • self-paced
  • interactive
  • company sponsored
  • interpersonal
  • team oriented.

Lest you also get carried away by wanting to impress, review this Buzz-Phrase Projector created by a former government employee who mocked the tendency to use nouns as adjectives, one on top of the next. Enjoy it—but, please, don't take Broughton's Phrase Projector seriously.

The Systematic Buzz-Phrase Projector

After years of hacking through etymological thickets at the U.S. Public Health Service, an official named Philip Broughton hit upon a surefire method for converting frustration into fulfillment. He euphemistically calls it the Systematic Buzz-Phrase Projector. Broughton's system employs a lexicon of thirty carefully chosen buzzwords.

The procedure is simple. Think of any three-digit number, then select the corresponding buzzword from each column. For instance, number 257 produces *systematized logistical projection*, a phrase that can be dropped into virtually any report to give it that ring of decisive, knowledgeable authority.

"People won't have the remotest idea of what you're talking about," says Broughton, "but the important thing is that they're not about to admit it."

Column 1	**Column 2**	**Column 3**
0. integrated	0. management	0. options
1. total	1. organizational	1. flexibility
2. systematized	2. monitored	2. capability
3. parallel	3. reciprocal	3. mobility
4. functional	4. digital	4. programming
5. responsive	5. logistical	5. concept
6. optional	6. transitional	6. time phase
7. synchronized	7. incremental	7. projection
8. compatible	8. third-generation	8. hardware
9. balanced	9. policy	9. contingency

4. GET RID OF DO-LITTLE VERBS AND PASSIVE VOICES

Verbs are the heartbeat of your sentences. If you choose strong ones, they'll vitalize your writing. Choose weak ones, and your sentences will struggle—as will your readers—to get to your point.

Lifeless Versus Life-Giving Verbs

Weak verbs do little. Concrete, active, picture verbs do much. In all its tenses, the most lifeless verb is the verb *to be*, creating "is-ness" in your writing.

> **"Is-ness" is a disease of dullness marked**
> **by weak use of forms of the verb** *to be*.

"Is-ness":	According to a recent poll, it was revealed . . .
Improved:	A recent poll revealed . . .
"Is-ness":	This tyrant, whose name is a blister to our tongue, was once thought honest.
Improved:	This tyrant, whose name blisters our tongue, was once thought honest.
"Is-ness":	Cutting our department's budget is another way to reduce morale.
Improved:	Cutting our department's budget also reduces morale.
"Is-ness":	I am in agreement with those who were in attendance at the meeting.
Improved:	I agree with those who attended.

Forms of the verb "to be" aren't the only culprits. They are joined by other do-little verbs contributing to dullness:

- make
- have
- go
- get
- come

Forms of these verbs add wordiness to your sentences and smother them with fat, as shown in the following examples.

Do-little Verb: The manager will make a decision next week.

Unsmothered: The manager will decide next week.

Do-Little Verb: I have a suspicion that the VP will resign.

Unsmothered: I suspect the VP will resign.

Do-Little Verb: The product manager will go to meet the marketing consultant next week.

Unsmothered: The product manager will meet the marketing consultant next week.

Do-Little Verb: The Sales Rep of the Year will get to have a meeting with the CEO.

Unsmothered: The Sales Rep of the Year will meet with the CEO.

Do-Little Verb: The division manager came to the conclusion the incentive would work.

Unsmothered: The division manager concluded the incentive would work.

When you use do-little verbs, you inadvertently weaken your writing because dull verbs require more nouns to support them, thus slowing down your sentences. Making verbs into nouns can also slow your pace. Examine your own writing to see if it is noun heavy. The presence of do-little verbs in your sentences is one warning sign. Word endings on your nouns is another. Particular word endings you can spot:

- -tion
- -ment
- -ance, - ancy
- -ity
- -ness

If your writing is overrun with these common suffixes, then you have converted many strong, action-packed verbs into nouns. Revise them and see if you don't like the smooth, swift word flow better. The following examples illustrate how noun-laden sentences can be resuscitated.

Smothered Verbs	*Resuscitated*
. . . provide an illustration . . .	illustrate
. . . it is our expectation . . .	we expect
. . . give a performance . . .	perform
. . . come to the realization . . .	realize
. . . carry out experiments . . .	experiment
. . . are found to be in agreement . . .	agree with
. . . will be of assistance to . . .	will help
John has the authorization . . .	John can
Jim initiated a confrontation . . .	Jim confronted
We reached a determination	We determined
The company provided employment . . .	The company employed
My boss made a concession..	My boss conceded
Anita gave consideration to . . .	Anita considered
People make suggestions . . .	People suggested
The company gave recognition to . . .	The company recognized
Everyone was in attendance . . .	Everyone attended
He made a choice . . .	He chose
The CEO put in an appearance . . .	The CEO appeared
The manager afforded an opportunity to . . .	The manager allowed
We made our departure . . .	We left
Sue made the statement that . . .	Sue stated/said
Steve has an ability to . . .	Steve can
The district manager gave positive encouragement to . . .	The district manager encouraged
The visiting VPs made their departure . . .	The visiting VPs departed/left
The product manager has a preference for . . .	The product manager prefers
The wholesalers' responses were an indication of . . .	The wholesalers' responses indicated/showed
The sales rep has a tendency to . . .	The sales rep tends

As you strive to liven your sentences with action verbs, be careful not to overdo it. The verb *directs* the sentence somewhere, but *too* many verbs in the same sentence direct the sentence nowhere. Instead, too many verbs fight with one another for control. Often readers give up because they have to work too hard to figure out what action is taking place. If you find any sentence (as in this example) with more than three verbs or verb phrases, weed out all but the real action verbs.

Too many verbs: I think you will find that our department is one that can handle the project you are adding.

Concise: Our department can handle your additional project.

What a weight loss! From *eighteen* words to seven. The pace of the sentence picks up as soon as you discard the symptoms of clutter—the "I ache," the "thatery," the "is-ness," and the "do-little" verbs. These symptoms only obscure your key ideas.

Sloppy verbs can also obscure your ideas. These are phrases, such as "would of," "could of," and "should of," that slip into our writing as a result of sloppy articulation and/or poor hearing. No such verb phrases exist, at least correctly. So listen and write more carefully: "Would have," "could have," and "should have" are legitimate. "Would of," "could of," "should of," not!

Active Versus Passive Voice

Overuse of the passive voice also contributes to dullness in business writing. While the passive voice is not wrong grammatically, it is cumbersome, wordy, and often unnecessarily vague. What *is* passive voice? What's the difference between these two sentences?

Passive: In the job-analysis study the following activities were completed.

Active: In the job-analysis study we completed the following activities.

Passive and active voice refer to the verb—the action—in a sentence. A passive construction shifts the subject, or *actor*, into a position following the verb—or *action*—or it can eliminate the actor entirely as in the first example above. (*Who* completed the activities?) In the active voice, the subject of the sentence is the agent of the verb's action. In the passive voice that intuitively logical relationship is upset, and the *object* of the action becomes the subject of the sentence.

Passive constructions provide some variety, but if you write with concise, active verbs, your writing will be clearer, more direct, more likely to accomplish your purpose—and shorter.

Passive: A profit loss of 10M was experienced by the brand.
Active: The brand lost 10M in profits.

Passive: A survey of customers' needs was undertaken by the division.
Active: The division surveyed customers' needs.

Passive: Jim was told by his manager to shape up.
Active: Jim's manager told him to shape up.

Passive: It was determined by the committee that . . .
Active: The committee determined that . . .

Consciously decide whether to use the active or passive voice. What—or who—is most important in the sentence? The grammar of the sentence reflects your decision simply because the subject of the sentence has more authority than the object.

Passive: The advantages and disadvantages of electing direct deposit are explained by the benefits administrator in the *Employee Bulletin*.

Active: The benefits administrator explains in the *Employee Bulletin* the advantages and disadvantages of electing direct deposit.

In the passive construction our attention is on the advantages and disadvantages (subject of the passive verb "are explained") rather than on who explains them. In the active construction the benefits administrator has moved to the subject position and thus has assumed the important position in the sentence.

Passive: The stock-option policy was changed more than a year ago.

Active: The board changed the stock-option policy more than a year ago.

In the passive construction the policy holds the prominent position in the sentence. In fact, who changed it is omitted. With the active construction the board becomes the subject and, in doing so, assumes the key spot.

Passive: The consultants were recommended by the Executive VP of Finance.

Active: The Executive VP of Finance recommended the consultants.

The consultants have the dominant position in the passive construction, whereas the Executive VP takes the prominent position in the active construction.

Use passive voice when . . .

- the "doer" is less important than the receiver:
  The new medical secretary was recommended by several doctors.

- the "doer" is neither known nor important:
  The wheel was invented thousands of years ago.

- you want to avoid identifying the "doer":
  The disrespectful employee was placed on disciplinary probation.

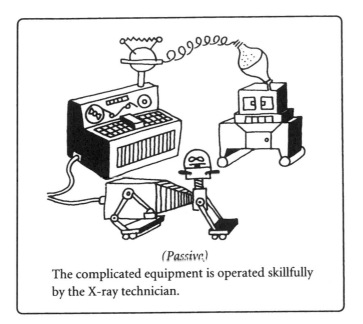

(Passive)
The complicated equipment is operated skillfully
by the X-ray technician.

In this passive construction the equipment appears in the subject position. Thus, we interpret that the equipment is more important than who operates it. In the active sentence, however, the technician assumes the important position as subject of the sentence. So you see, it all depends on what you as the writer want to stress.

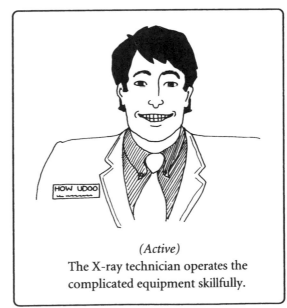

(Active)
The X-ray technician operates the
complicated equipment skillfully.

See how you can stress what you want in the following examples by changing
from passive to active.

(Passive)
The layout for the new building
was designed by Sheila Taylor.

(Active)
Sheila Taylor designed the layout
for the new building.

(Passive)
The truck can be repaired by the
mechanic.

(Active)
The mechanic can repair the truck.

(Passive)
The report was written by the president.

OR

(Active)
The president wrote the report.

(Passive)
The truck was driven off the road.

OR

(Active)
The driver drove the truck off the road.

5. DELETE DULL INTENSIFIERS

■ rather	■ totally
■ more	■ extremely
■ very	■ slightly
■ really	■ basically
■ utterly	■ probably
■ somewhat	■ sort of/kind of
■ mostly	■ quite

These words *basically* add *very* little to *really* distinguish your writing from other *rather* poor examples. If you cannot *utterly* reject these words before they hit paper, strike them out as you revise. Instead of *somewhat* intensifying your meaning, these words *sort of* bloat your sentences, *probably* diluting the essence of the word that follows each intensifier.

These dull intensifiers abound in advertising, in sports, and in talk. So, it's little wonder people use them without realizing they're unnecessary. In the previous sentence, *little* has a purpose, while in the following examples, the intensifiers add no substance. In fact, they weaken, not intensify, the writing by making it come across as tentative. Simply removing the intensifier in each sentence will create a more confident-sounding tone.

■ I was really surprised at the number of pages we had when I kept track.
■ Basically, taxes are figured in the same manner.
■ This would probably apply to you also.
■ The manager was really concerned when John was so extremely late this morning.
■ Tom pursued his job search quite aggressively and somewhat successfully.

If you find yourself relying heavily on intensifiers, it may be symptomatic of an unsuccessful struggle to locate the "right" word. Instead, you settle on the intensifier to help out. Try removing the intensifier to see if the word it was intensifying can work alone in the sentence. If it's not quite right, turn to your thesaurus. And remember Ben Franklin's thriftiness: "Never use two words where one will do."

Instead of	Write
very stubborn	obstinate, unmovable
very late	unpunctual, overdue
very convenient	suitable, opportune
very amazing	incredible
very weak	feeble, frail
very stupid	absent-minded, naive
very appreciative	beholden, grateful
very quiet	still, silent
very happy	joyful, ecstatic
very pretty	attractive, beautiful
very antagonistic	hostile
very alive	vivacious, spirited
very small	tiny, slight
very large	enormous, immense, huge, spacious, vast
very angry	enraged, indignant
very far	distant, remote
very near	adjacent, close
very hot	torrid, scorching, fiery
very cold	frigid, icy, arctic
very surprised	astonished, amazed
very loud	thunderous, deafening, emphatic, earsplitting
very common	hackneyed, ordinary, trite
very strong	powerful, potent
very hard	strenuous, difficult

6. ELIMATE PREPOSITIONAL FILLERS

POLONIUS:	*What do you read, my lord?*
HAMLET:	*Words, words, words.*

Shakespeare, *Hamlet*

Prepositions, those pesky little words that we could never memorize in school: with, on, under, over, by, in, at, near, etc. They're back! Hunt them down in your sentences, and if they or the phrases they're attached to can be excised, do so!

Here are several examples to jog your memory.

Too Many Words	*Improved*
Something's rotten *in the state* of Denmark	Something's rotten *in* Denmark.
The thrust of this program was to combat complacency *in conjunction with* retailer service.	The program's goal was to combat complacency *in* retailer service.
Thank you for inviting me to speak to you *on the topic of* our manufacturing process.	Thank you for inviting me to speak to you *about* our manufacturing process.
. . . a copy of our check requisition *in the amount of* $228 . . .	. . . a copy of our check requisition *for* $228 . . .
I was thoroughly impressed with his qualifications *in terms of our search for* a sales-rep candidate.	I was impressed with his qualifications *for* sales rep.
With respect to our distributors, their incentive benefits will be void during the fourth quarter.	Distributors' incentive benefits will be void during the fourth quarter.
During the month of April . . .	*During* April . . .
Between the years of 2000 and 2010 . . .	*Between* 2000 and 2010 . . .
despite the fact that	*although*
in view of the fact that	*because*
during the course of	*during*
on an annual basis	*annually*
in the majority of instances	*usually*
with reference to	*about*
in many cases	*often*
in the event that	*if*
at this point in time	*now*
for the purpose of	*to*
due to the fact that	*because*
in the final analysis	*finally*
in order that	*so*
in the course of	*while*
until such time as	*until*
in conjunction with	*with*

7. EXCISE IMPRECISE AND AMBIGUOUS LANGUAGE

It's not enough to write so you are understood. You must write so you cannot possibly be misunderstood. Imprecise language can be easily misinterpreted. Have a look:

> The processes have been put into motion to
> make the candidate more marketable.

What processes? Did the candidate shave, buy a new suit, get a toupee?

> Can you get these to me within a few days?

Your idea of a "few" days may not coincide with someone else's.

> . . . attended our workshop and quickly
> located another job.

Who gets to define what's "quick"?

> . . . due to an unavoidable delay.

Was it a broken leg, a downed computer, a company reorganization?

Imprecise Language

Vague words fall short of convincing your audience. Readers want specifics. But being precise doesn't require long-windedness. Often one exact word replaces the imprecise one.

Imprecise	*Specific*
We have your recent letter.	We have your May 2 letter.
Please send us a supply of pamphlets for distribution.	Please send 500 pamphlets for us to distribute.
You can count on our quick turnaround.	You can count on our 24-hour turnaround.
The sampling was a huge success.	The sampling served more than 3,000 people.
The chain is very willing to have us build displays.	The chain requested displays be set up by March 2.

So why aren't more writers precise? Sometimes it's pure laziness. More often, however, being specific requires a writer's taking responsibility—and being responsible. It's no wonder staying vague is the more popular choice. But beware. If you choose imprecision, your writing will lack confidence and persuasiveness.

Strive to be precise. Your writing will reflect confidence and knowledge.

Imprecise	*Specific*
a sizable loss	a 34-percent loss
work-saving machine	performs the work of five employees
monitoring sales on a regular basis	monitoring sales weekly
in the near future	by June
extenuating circumstance	a broken leg
as soon as possible	by the 15th
saves you money	$200-per-year savings
She is a good employee.	She learns quickly and can train new employees.
a better position	a 25-percent increase in profits
a gradual increase	a 20-percent yearly gain over the last five years
unsanitary conditions	food served on dirty dishes
the present writer	I
a draught-equipment malfunction	a clogged tap
a slight reduction	two cents off each bottle
meet with you soon	on July 1
finish the plan as soon as possible	by the third quarter

The Free-Agent This

The free-floating *this* is a frequent contributor to ambiguity. Often it hovers over a sentence, and you are never quite sure what word it intended to land alongside. For example:

> The town officials watched as the new government center's doors opened for the first time. This was the first evidence of the township's plans for expansion.

This does not quickly make plain what the evidence is: the door's opening? The officials present? It would be clearer to say:

> This building was the first evidence of the township's plans for expansion.

Here's another example:

> The week offers activities that attempt to raise consciousness regarding illegal and abusive use of our products. This provides the perfect opportunity to convey our view to the audience.

Does *this* refer to the illegal and abusive use of our products? I hope not! It would be clearer to say:

> This week provides the perfect opportunity to have our voice heard.

Ambiguous Language

When a writer uses vague language, the reader is unclear, fuzzy about what the writer's real intention was. Similarly, ambiguous language leaves the reader in the dark as to which of several, competing meanings is intended.

Hmm . . . is the speaker for or against the candidate?

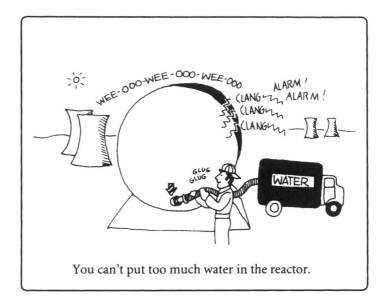

You can't put too much water in the reactor.

Hmm . . . a reader might misinterpret this to mean the more water, the better!

We need more competent salespeople.

Hmm . . . do we already have a competent staff and just need more of them? Or do we have a bunch of idiots?

Visiting managers can be boring.

Hmm . . . both interpretations might be appropriate!

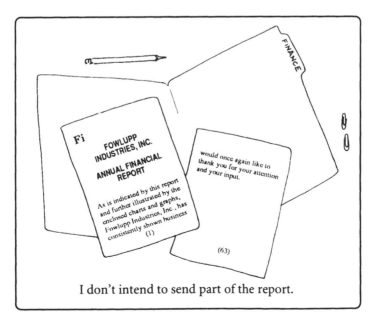

I don't intend to send part of the report.

Hmm . . . are you sending all of it then?

Ambiguous Exercise

Rewrite these sentences and remove any competing meanings.

1. The VP told his colleague that he had the board's approval.
   Revision: _____

2. Your letter and request arrived today, but we cannot ship it until next week.
   Revision: _____

3. Emma Brain almost recovered all the misplaced funds.
   Revision: _____

4. Inadequate customer service has caused a serious market-share loss. This is our biggest problem at the moment.
   Revision: _____

Suggested Rewrites

1. The VP, having received the board's approval, shared the news with his colleague.

2. Your letter and request arrived today. We will ship the supplies next week.

3. Emma Brain recovered almost all the misplaced funds.

4. Inadequate customer service has caused a serious market-share loss. This poor service is our biggest problem at the moment.

8. BANISH PRETENTIOUS LANGUAGE

> *Nor use too swelling or ill-sounding words.*
> Ben Jonson

Pretentious language is the language of jargon, foreign phrases, multi-syllabic words, legalese, corporatese, euphemese, and vogue words. Stop yourself from the temptation to pad your writing with such clutter.

> *The source of bad writing is the desire to be something more than a person of sense—the straining to be thought a genius. If people would only say what they have to say in plain terms, how much more eloquent they would be.*
> Samuel Taylor Coleridge

Jargon	*Plain Language*
viable alternatives	alternatives, possibilities
commensurate	equal to
facilitate	help
scenario	possibility
optimize	enhance, improve
incentivize	reward, encourage, pay

Sometimes the longer word *will* be the best, but opt more often for the shorter. Don't get carried away with "-izing" or "-wising" as did Jack Lemmon when he stated in the classic film "The Apartment," "That's the way it crumbles, cookiewise."

Instead of	*Use*
optimum	best
subsequent	next
verification	proof
cessation	stop, pause

> *I am a Bear of very little Brain, and long words bother me.*
> A. A. Milne, a.k.a. Winnie the Pooh

Avoid dropping foreign phrases into your writing in an effort to sound intelligent. Such phrases are nothing more than "phony fancies."

Foreign Terms	*Translation*
bona fide	genuine
carte blanche	authority, full rein
fait accompli	a done deed
faux pas	blunder, mistake
joie de vivre	joy of/zest for life
milieu	surroundings
modus operandi	method
nonpareil	without match
non sequitur	illogical
per annum	yearly
per diem	daily
per se	as such
raison d'être	primary reason for, justification for
sans	without
sine qua non	essential

Many phrases of foreign origin, in particular, per annum and per diem, are now widely used in the workplace. In fact, *Webster's* includes all the words in this list of foreign phrases without requiring they be italicized as foreign. Even so, my point concerns your intention in using such words or phrases when you write: Is it to impress or is it to communicate clearly?

To win the battle of the bulge—in your writing, that is—employ this strategy: Refuse inflated, highfalutin language.

"Then why study vocabulary in school?" you ask. Having an extensive word bank helps you select the *right* word to convey meaning—not necessarily the *biggest* word. The goal in business communication is to *express* information, not impress others with a fancy vocabulary. Familiar words, which are often simpler words, are processed by the brain more quickly. Inflated language distances your reader from you: It tires and confuses, alienates and angers. After all, which is easier to understand?

> During the course of the above-referenced project, data was developed and subjected to rigorous computer modeling which suggest that the system will, within specified parameters, produce viable results.
>
> *or*
>
> We tested it and it works.

W. H. Weiss, author of a management guide called *The Art and Skill of Managing People*, tells this amusing story about the consequences of inflated language.

Thinking that the Internal Revenue Service might be persuaded to extend the deadline for his income-tax payment, an individual sent the IRS a letter requesting an extension. Two weeks later he received this answer: "The Internal Revenue Service does not assume a panegyrical, eulogistic, or encomiastic viewpoint toward the delay of remittance of tax due the government."

Interpreting this statement as granting permission, the taxpayer wrote back to thank the government: "I am pleased to learn it is okay for me to pay my tax a month late. Thank you."

Realizing there was a misunderstanding, the IRS immediately wrote a second letter: "The postponement of tax payment is interdictive action and will be abnegated by the government authority."

The taxpayer acknowledged the second letter: "Thank you again for allowing me another month. It will save me some money."

The IRS sent a third letter: "You must pay by April 15. We'll fine you if you don't."

It took a while, but the government finally understood what Dartmouth professor David Lambuth meant back in 1923 when he wrote, "Although there is much mistaken opinion to the contrary, literary English does not demand a stiff, stilted Latinistic vocabulary. It demands the simplest words, the most familiar words, the most concrete words consistent with accurate expression and good everyday usage." We'd do well to heed his words today.

Pretentious Words Are Everywhere!

Is there another, shorter, and unstuffy way to say it?

Avoid Saying	*When You Mean*
acceded	agreed
accommodate	serve
acquire	get
advise	tell, write
affirmative	yes
am in possession of	have, possess
anticipate	expect
approximately	about
ascertain	find out
attempt	try
cognizant	know, aware
commencing	starting, beginning
compel	make
complete	fill out
concerning	about
cooperate	work with
deem	think
desire	want
determine	find out
effect	make
endeavor	try
ensuing	following
execute	do, sign
expedite	rush
facilitate	ease, aid, foster
forward, furnish	send

Avoid Saying	*When You Mean*
generate	make, cause
illustrate	show
inaugurate	begin
indicate	say
initial	first
in lieu of	instead
inquire	ask
kindly	please
locate	find
methodology	methods, way
numerous	many
observe	see, watch
obtain	get
occurs	happens
operate	do
originated	began
personnel	people
peruse	read
precipitated	caused
predicated	based on
prior to	before
procure	get, take
pursuant to	under
recapitulate	sum up
remainder	rest
remunerate	pay
render	give, send
represents	is
request	ask
require	need
retain	keep
reveal	show
review	check
said item	the item
solicit	ask
stated	said

Avoid Saying	*When you Mean*
submit	send
subsequent to	after
sufficient	enough
supply	send
terminate	end, quit
thus	so, therefore
transpire	happen, occur
utilize	use
vacate	leave
vehicle	car, van

Pretentious Phrases Are Everywhere, Too

Stuffy	*Suggested Substitute*
acknowledge receipt of (*as in* "We *acknowledge receipt of* the data.")	Thank you for your data.
advise (as in "We *advise* you that shipment has . . .")	inform
allow me to (*as in "Allow me to* express our appreciation . . .")	thank you
answer in the affirmative	*say yes; agree*
as a matter of fact	*Omit this phrase.*
as per	according to
at all times	always
at an early date	soon, *or give exact date*
at hand (*as in* "We have your letter *at hand.*")	*Omit this phrase.*
at a later date	later, *or give exact date*
at the present time	now
Attached please find; Enclosed please find	Enclosed is . . . *or*, We are enclosing . . .
at that time	then
at your earliest convenience	soon, *or give exact date*

Stuffy	_Suggested Substitute_
awaiting your favor	I/we hope to hear from you soon. Or, Please let me/us hear from you soon.
beg (_as in_ "_beg_ to inform," "_beg_ to state")	_Omit; go ahead and inform or state._
by means of	by
contents duly noted	thank you
despite the fact that	though, although
due to the fact that	because
favor (_as in_ "In your _favor_ of October 22 . . .")	letter
for the purpose of	to, for
for the reason that	since, because
for your information	_Omit this phrase._
in accordance with your request	as you requested
in addition	also
in the amount of (_as in_ "our check _in the amount of . . ._")	our check for
inasmuch as	since
in the event that	if, in case
in the nature of	like
in the near future	soon, _or give exact date_
in the neighborhood of	about
in the normal course of our procedure	normally
in order that	so
in order to	to
in this connection	_Omit this phrase._
in this day and age	today
in view of the fact that	because
I/we are not in a position to	I/we cannot
I/we regret to inform you that	I/we are sorry that/for
of the order of magnitude of	about

Stuffy	*Suggested Substitute*
on the grounds that	because
on the occasion of	when, on
permit me to say	*Omit (go ahead and say it).*
prior to	before
pursuant to our agreement	as we agreed
the reason is due to	because
recent date	*Give exact date.*
subsequent to	after
thanking you in advance	I/we will appreciate any information you may care to send.
thank you kindly	thank you
This letter is for the purpose of	*Why all this preliminary? Go ahead and ask.*
this will acknowledge receipt of your letter	*Omit this phrase.*
under date of	on
under separate cover	by FedEx, *or whatever means of sending*
(the) undersigned	I/we
up to this writing	previously
We would like to ask that	please
will you be kind enough to	please
wish to acknowledge	*Omit this phrase.*
with a view to	to
without further delay	now, immediately
with reference to	about
with regard to	about
with respect to	about
with the result that	so that
the writer(s)	I, we
you claim, you state	*Rewrite in order to omit.*
yours (*as in "Yours* of recent date")	your letter, your report *(Be specific.)*

Legalese	*Suggested Substitute*
pursuant to your instructions issued heretofore	as you instructed
A summary of the background of the candidate is enclosed herewith.	A summary of the candidate's background is enclosed.
in compliance with your memorandum, which we are in receipt of	to cooperate regarding/in response to the memo we received
the aforementioned case	the Bergen case
relative to the above-captioned subject, this wishes to state that	*Omit, and simply state your point.*

Corporatese	*Suggested Substitute*
as I mentioned to you via our phone conversation	as I mentioned during our phone conversation
We wish to maximize our earning potential and optimize our marketing strategies.	*Omit the "izes."* We wish to build our earning potential and develop peerless marketing strategies.
As per John's memo, several events impacted consumer buying habits last quarter.	As John stated, several events altered consumer buying habits last quarter.

Euphemese	*The Real Meaning*
contrary to expectations	We sure didn't predict this one!
revenue enhancement	taxes or price increases
negative impact	bad effect
moonlight specials	red-eye flights
the Peacekeeper	MX missile
negative growth	We lost money!
limited success	failure
downsizing, right-sizing, decruiting	layoffs
challenges, opportunities	problems

Here's a game that mocks the use of "in vogue" words. Try playing "Buzzword Bingo" at your next management meeting. First seen on the Internet, the original Buzzword Bingo has been attributed to several sources, among them Dilbert's creator, Scott Adams. But you can make up your own cards, as I did here by creating a list of words being overused in the office.

Here's how to play: Each time someone uses one of these "vogue" words or phrases in a meeting, cross it off—and see how quickly you get "Bingo." Best be quiet, however, when you do. After all, the buzzword-spouting expert may not appreciate being the target of such playful sarcasm.

Buzzword Bingo				
PARADIGMS	PROCESSES	STRATEGIES	PROACTIVE	EDGE
ACTION PLANS	INTERACTIVE	SYNERGISTIC	CLIENT-BASED	TEAMWORK
LEADERSHIP	HORIZONTAL ORGANIZA-TIONS	WILD CARD (any acronym)	EMPOWERING	INTERFACE
RIGHTSIZE	BUSINESS CASE	INITIATIVES	NETWORKING DELIVER-ABLES	ACTUALIZE
VISION	INFORMATION HIGHWAY	FLATTENING	CUSTOMER-DRIVEN	PARTNERING

Pretension-Busting Exercise

In the event that you may be desirous of here and now utilizing your hereinafter expertise, if it so please you, indulge in these exercises and eliminate any traces of pretension. *Merci beaucoup!*

1. **Pretentious:** He has great *joie de vivre.*

   Plain: _____

2. **Pretentious:** We discussed what had occurred heretofore.

   Plain: _____

3. **Pretentious:** The equipment was operational.

   Plain: _____

4. **Pretentious:** What was the output of the incentivization efforts?

   Plain: _____

5. **Pretentious:** The managers interfaced with the team about the parameters of the team's responsibility.

   Plain: _____

Suggested Rewrites

1. He has enthusiasm for life.
2. We discussed what had occurred up to/until now.
3. The equipment worked.
4. What were the results of the incentive?
5. The managers talked with the team about the limits of the team's responsibility.

9. REDUCE REDUNDANCY

The most valuable of all talents is that of never using two words where one will do.
Thomas Jefferson

Knowledgeable experts advise *never, ever* using *redundant words and verbiage*. Redundancies are *unnecessary and useless*. They clutter your writing by *repeating over and over again* what you've already said. So *face up to* it now rather than *postpone until later*. *Eliminate completely* these needless goofs. Remember, your *ultimate goal* is to write clearly and concisely.

Naturally, some redundancies can be spotted immediately, *without close scrutiny*. Others are not as easy to find because they occur so often in *normal, everyday* speech and writing. As a result, they sound *perfectly legitimate*. But they're not. They *seriously hamper* your professionalism and originality. So, make a *major breakthrough*. Let your *past experience* guide you to a *definite decision* to do better in *verbal and oral* matters. Unnecessary repetition adds empty length and weakens the power of the single word.

Easier said than done? Indeed, it is often harder to boil down than to write. Harder, yes; impossible, no.

But how did so many needless words end up in our writing? One reason is that we've forgotten (or have never learned) what particular words mean. A second reason: Too many of us took Oscar Wilde seriously when he said, "Nothing succeeds like excess."

In the struggle to make a point, business writers often overmake it by using more words than needed. So how do you whittle your words? Writer Sydney Smith quipped, "In composing, as a general rule, run your pen through every other word that you have written; you have no idea what vigor it will give your style." While Smith's method may not be that far awry, removing deadwood isn't quite so simple as striking out every other word! But here's a strategy that will work:

Think about what each word means. Make every word work in a sentence. If it doesn't contribute, remove it. But remember that some repetition is useful, even essential, for rhythm and/or emphasis, as in these examples:

- "First in war—first in peace—and first in the hearts of his countrymen . . ."
  —*Henry Lee* in funeral oration for George Washington
- "Too kind—too kind."—*Florence Nightingale* when handed the insignia of the Order of Merit on her deathbed

- "What had to be done was done."—*Charles de Gaulle*
- "The life so short, the craft so long to learn."—*Hippocrates*
- ". . . the old, old words worn thin, defaced by ages of careless usage."—Joseph Conrad

In contrast, the following list you can prune easily. When you do, you'll give your sentences the power and lift they need to fly.

Redundant	*Concise*
absolutely complete	complete
active consideration	consideration
actual truth	truth
adequate enough	adequate
advance warning	warning
agreeable and satisfactory	*Use just one.*
and etc.	etc.
anxious and eager	*Use just one.*
assemble together	assemble
at about	about
background experience	*Use just one.*
basic fundamentals	fundamentals
big in size	big
both alike	alike
cancel out	cancel
check into	check
classify into groups	classify
climb up	climb
close proximity	proximity
collaborate together	collaborate
commute back and forth	commute
complete monopoly	monopoly
completely filled	filled
component parts	components
consensus of opinion	consensus
continue on	continue
cooperate together	cooperate
count up	count
courteous and polite	*Use just one.*
customary practice	practice
definitely interested	interested
depreciate in value	depreciate

Redundant	*Concise*
divide in two	divide
doctorate degree	doctorate
during the course of	during
each and every one of us	each of us, every one of us, all of us
endorse on the back	endorse
end result	result
equally as well	equally
exactly identical	identical
exact replica	replica
face up to	face
few in number	few
filled to capacity	filled
final completion	completion
first and foremost	*Use just one.*
follow after	follow
foreign import	import
free gift	gift
full and complete	*Use just one.*
future plans	plans
heir apparent	heir
honest opinion	opinion
hope and trust	hope
if and when	*Use just one.*
in four weeks' time	in four weeks
inside of	inside
insist and demand	*Use just one.*
invited guest	guest
join together	join
later on	later
latest status report	status
lift up	lift
lose out	lose
major breakthrough	breakthrough
make perfectly clear	make clear
may perhaps	may
merge together	merge
mutual agreement	agreement
my personal opinion	my opinion
near to	near

Redundant	*Concise*
new beginner	beginner
null and void	*Use just one.*
off of	off
old adage	adage
open up	open
original source	source
over with	over
passing fad	fad
past experience	experience
past history	*Use just one.*
personal friend	friend
p]ever	rarely
reason is because	reason is
red in color	red
refer back to	refer to
revert back	revert
right and proper	*Use just one.*
root cause	*Use just one.*
round in shape	round
seal off	seal
seldom ever	seldom
serious danger	danger
seriously consider	consider
sincere and earnest	*Use just one.*
sink down	sink
successful achievement	achievement
temporary loan	loan
temporary reprieve	reprieve
thoroughly examine	examine
thought and consideration	*Use just one.*
true facts	facts
try out	try
undergraduate student	undergraduate
unexpected emergency	emergency
unique (*as in* "the most *unique,*" "very *unique*")	Unique *means one of a kind, without equal; use it by itself.*
unsubstantiated rumors	rumors
usual custom	custom
utterly reject	reject

Redundant	*Concise*
visit with	visit
wall mural	mural
whether or not	whether
8 P.M. in the evening	8 P.M.

Redundancy-Cutting Exercise

Eliminate the redundancies in these sentences and make them concise.

1. **Redundant:** As soon as I receive their response, I will immediately circulate it for Functional Review.

   Concise:_____

2. **Redundant:** Before Mike approves the attached purchase order, it has to
   go to the department head first.

   Concise:_____

3. **Redundant:** By giving that little bit of extra effort, it will help keep us in
   the number one position.

   Concise:_____

4. **Redundant:** At the current time, our retailers are now involved in the ad
   campaign.

   Concise:_____

5. **Redundant:** He is an expert in the area of market research.

   Concise:_____

6. **Redundant:** Worried about the legality factor, we sent the promotion
   agreement to Legal for approval.

   Concise:_____

(continued)

Redundancy-Cutting Exercise (continued)

7. **Redundant:** There were several openings in the field of Marketing.

    Concise:_____

8. **Redundant:** We have a problem with this media thing/issue.

    Concise:_____

9. **Redundant:** We discussed some real instances that actually happened to the sales force.

    Concise:_____

10. **Redundant:** Two out of three of our competitors both have been using the new technology.

    Concise:_____

Suggested Rewrites

1. As soon as I receive their response, I will circulate it for functional review.

2. Before Mike approves the attached purchase order, it has to go to the department head.

3. That extra effort will keep us number one.

4. Our retailers are involved in the ad campaign.

5. He is a market-research expert.

6. Worried, we sent the promotion agreement to Legal for approval.

7. Marketing has several openings.

8. We have a problem with unsympathetic reporting *or* with the media.

9. We discussed real examples.

10. Two of our three competitors have been using the new technology.

10. Cut Out Clichéd Openings and Closings . . . and In-Betweens

Let me state my case against these and other opening clichés. You have only one chance to make that first, good impression—in your business writing as well as in your speaking. Your opening is your opportunity to telegraph to an often impatient audience your conciseness, clarity, capability, and originality.

Are there guidelines for creating that first, positive impression of yourself in the opening of your letter, memo, or report? Indeed, and here are a few.

- **Subordinate references to previous conversations and correspondence.** Don't start with "This is in reference to your correspondence dated June 28." Why? A reference is not the major point of your letter. Work it in, but don't begin with it. Busy readers prefer hearing the bottom line up front. Long, stale introductions waste time and frazzle nerves.

  Not   Dear Mr. George:

  This confirms our phone conversation on June 20 in regard to our July 2 meeting with Haynes, Inc., to discuss the new compensation policy.

  Instead, try this: Dear Mr. George:

  Thank you for agreeing to attend our July 2 meeting with Haynes, Inc., to discuss the new compensation policy. As I mentioned during our phone conversation, we would like your reaction to the salary ranges for the engineers in your department.

The latter opening gives Mr. George precise information. He'll thank you for putting the bottom line right at the start and appreciate your style.

- **Avoid overused openers that have become clichés.** Using them gives your writing a stale sound and a rubber-stamp quality. Retire these:

  - I am pleased to inform you . . .
  - It has come to my attention . . .
  - Per your memo . . .
  - This is in response to your request of . . .

- Reference is made to our recent conversation . . .
- Regarding your letter of . . .
- This is in reference to our telephone conversation concerning . . .
- In reference to our meeting last week . . .

- **Avoid "enclosure" statements as a way to begin.**
  Like their formulaic counterparts above, they are mechanical. And if you've remembered to enclose it, your reader will find it! Omit opening with

First, I'd like to say . . .
Second, it should be mentioned . . .
Third, etc., etc., etc. . . .

  - Enclosed please find . . .
  - Attached is . . .
  - Enclosed herewith . . .
  - Attached hereto . . .

  (These last two not only make your writing sound legalistic, but are also redundant.) Instead, start by telling your reader *why* you've enclosed or attached something— the value of the enclosure.

- **Avoid opening statements that suggest a point but don't indicate your position on it.**

  > Waiting until the fourth quarter to raise prices on the new product line is an idea to consider.

  Do you believe it's a good idea? If so, say so!

  > I recommend raising prices on the new product line during the fourth quarter.

- **Avoid opening with social comments.**

  > Hope the kids are fine and that the house renovation is complete.

While this may be nice to say, it's unnecessary in business correspondence.

The best openings are simple and direct. They are confident and contain concrete information. The writer uses them to take a stand rather than hedging or being wishy-washy or trite. "In regard to our telephone conversation on May 18 . . ." is an unnecessarily long and imprecise windup leading to your point. "I agree that we should market our product internationally . . ." says it quickly, vigorously.

Try for that vigor and directness unless you have a compelling reason for not putting your point up front—as in the case of writing to a reader who has a strong negative bias toward what you are saying. Then you may legitimately lead your reader more slowly to your point of view. But don't bore or insult her or him with tired, cardboard opening statements.

CLOSING CLICHÉS

While you're improving your openings, consider your closings. They're your last chance to leave readers with an impression of your value and the importance of your topic. Make your closings as concise and sincere as your openings. State a precise next step, a due date, if necessary, and offer a comment of good will. Avoid closings like the following ones which have become clichés. If you can't retire them, at least streamline them.

Avoid Closing Clichés	*Instead, try*
▪ Should you have any questions or require further assistance, please do not hesitate to contact me.	▪ As always, please call me if you have questions.
▪ If you have any further questions or comments, please do not hesitate to contact me.	▪ Please let me know if you need anything.
▪ Thank you for your help in this matter.	▪ Thanks for your help.
▪ Thanking you in advance for your cooperation.	▪ Thank you. *or* Thanks.
▪ Thank you for your attention to this matter.	▪ Our presence in the marketplace is ever growing, thanks to your efforts.
▪ Your prompt attention will be appreciated.	▪ Your response by (*date*) will ensure the accuracy of my report.
▪ . . . at your earliest convenience.	▪ . . . by (*date*).

The Cliché Finder

Once colorful, these clichés now drain your writing and speech of original thought. Here are many of the feeblest.

abreast of the times	bitter end	considered opinion
add insult to injury	bone of contention	coping well
agree to disagree	built-in safeguards	crying need
all things being equal	burning issues	curiously enough
all things considered	by the same token	
along these lines		diamond in the rough
ample opportunity	capacity crowd	dramatic new move
as a matter of fact	caught between a rock	drastic action
at a loss for words	and a hard place	due consideration
at long last	chain reaction	
at the end of the day	checkered career	eager for feedback
	circumstances beyond	eminently successful
benefit of the doubt	my control	equal to the occasion
better late than never	city fathers	exception to the rule

The Cliché Finder (continued)

exercise in futility	generation gap	iron out the difficulty
existing conditions	give the green light to	it goes without saying
	goes without saying	
final analysis	grave concern	just desserts
festive occasion		
few well-chosen words	heated argument	keep options open
finishing touches	Herculean efforts	
food for thought		leave no stone
foregone conclusions	in no uncertain	unturned
from the ridiculous	terms	leaves much to be
to the sublime	in short supply	desired
from time immemorial	in this day and age	leave well enough alone

. . . by the same token

The Cliché Finder (continued)

lend a helping hand

lesson for us all

line of least resistance

long-felt need

marked contrast

moment of truth

more than meets
   the eye

narrow escape

needless to say

needs no introduction

one and the same

on more than one
   occasion

open to new experiences

other things being
   equal

own worst enemy

paramount importance

part and parcel

pay the piper

piece of cake

pros and cons

put on the back burner

ready and willing

ready for the acid test

regrettable incident

reliable source

remedy the situation

ripe old age

rise to the occasion

round of applause

second to none

see if it flies

seek the meaning of life

select few

selling like hotcakes

stay the course

stick to our guns

sweeping changes

too numerous to
   mention

to tell the truth

unprecedented
   situation

untimely end

viable alternative

view with alarm

wave of the future

whole new ball game

wide open spaces

win-win situation

words fail me

worst-case scenario

Although clichés make writing and speech dreary, you can use them as stepping stones (oops . . . pardon the cliché) to create fresher language, as did John Caldwell here.

Untried and True

by John Caldwell

Do you find the old clichés a little, well, trite? Try these new and improved clichés:

- ✓ It's no paint off my fender.
- ✓ That's neither Barbie nor Ken.
- ✓ There is no free brunch.
- ✓ All that glitters is not dry.
- ✓ You'll catch more flies with honey than with Velcro.
- ✓ The early dog gets the worm.
- ✓ Don't cry over split peas.
- ✓ There are other clams in the chowder.
- ✓ No two ways about it, there are two sides to every story.
- ✓ More fun than a barrel of money.
- ✓ He's fruitier than a fruitcake.
- ✓ Keep your nose to the Flintstones.
- ✓ He can't see the hors d'oeuvres for the toothpicks.
- ✓ If you can't stand the heat, get out of the oven.
- ✓ Don't tell me I stink till you've walked a mile in my socks.
- ✓ Every straitjacket has a silver lining.
- ✓ The world is my mussel.
- ✓ What goes up must calm down.
- ✓ A man's reach should exceed his graft.
- ✓ Gasping on straws.
- ✓ You're the Kahlúa in my coffee.

Samuel Goldwyn (of Metro-Goldwyn-Mayer) was also clever at changing the familiar. Here are a few of his "Goldwynisms."

- "I'll give you a definite maybe."
- "Include me out."
- "I may not always be right, but I'm never wrong."
- "Tell me now, how did you love my picture?"

Yogi Berra has given us some original turns-of-phrase, too:

- "It ain't over till it's over."
- "You can observe a lot by watching."
- "Ninety-nine percent of this game is half mental."

So, too, did entertainer Danny Thomas:

- "Truth is shorter than fiction."

And Woody Allen:

- "I am at two with nature."

And might we say the following about several of our presidents:

- He never met a tax he didn't hike!
- A man is known by the company he avoids.

The key, then, is to take the hackneyed and make it new. And if that's not the truth, then I'm a monkey's aunt!

Cliché-Rewriting Exercise

Here's a "worst-case scenario"—a memo larded with clichés. Please give it your "due consideration." Keeping its intent, rewrite it, replacing its clichéd cant with original, fresh talk.

To: The Sales Force
From: Jess Desserts
Re: Better Selling in the Eleventh Hour

In this day and age it goes without saying that we are often caught between a rock and a hard place in this crowded global marketplace. The burning issues we must face will involve dramatic, proactive new moves from us to rise to the occasion, to add fuel to the fire, and to remedy the situation. To stay the course ahead of our competition won't be a piece of cake. So put on your thinking caps and come prepared for our meeting next week—we'll put our heads together and synergize to come up with a good plan of attack. See you then.

Suggested Rewrite to Compare with Yours

To: The Frontline Warriors
From: Jess Original
Re: Get Ready for Better Selling Rally,
          or Something's Rotten in ILL-inois

For our meeting 20 August, please arrive with suggestions we can incorporate into a tight defense plan. We need one because the competition is enjoying a sudden, unexpected second wind in the state. In fact, it's reaching gale forces. So it's time to question—and alter—our plans for the coming quarter if we want to keep our rivals at a respectable distance.

10
Tempering Your Tone

Life is not so short but that there is always time for courtesy.
Ralph Waldo Emerson

CONSIDERING YOUR READER, YOURSELF, AND YOUR TONE

Brevity and directness in business correspondence are, of course, important—but not at the cost of courtesy and personality. Even in the most routine writing tasks, you can—and should—build in personality and politeness. And though much business writing is formulaic, the most successful memos are written by people who understand that creativity and personality have a place in business and who are confident enough to infuse their writing with their own voice. According to E. B. White in the classic *The Elements of Style*, "No writer long remains incognito." With a little practice, you can sound like yourself *and* represent your organization well.

And while courtesy is common sense, it, like personality, is a principle frequently omitted in writing and speech. Yet both are crucial to elicit cooperation from your audience. To neglect the importance of a memo as an agent of goodwill, even in messages that say no, is to play the ostrich, head stuck in the sand.

So while it's important to write concisely and clearly, it's also important to establish common ground with your reader by stating your message in a tone and with a personality that won't distract your reader from your message.

The atmosphere your words create is tone—and an appropriate tone is an essential element of a business writer's style. When talking, you may use harsh words, but a joking tone can still be expressed through your smile, inflection, body language. In writing, you have only the words and their arrangement to do the job for you. So while a memo may be *correctly* written, it may not accomplish its purpose because of its tone. An appropriate tone will not write *up* or *down* to a reader but rather *to* that reader. And the tone will be appropriate to the subject as well as to the reader. Consider the atmosphere your words create and keep in mind these suggestions as well as Lincoln's advice: "What kills a skunk is the publicity it gives itself."

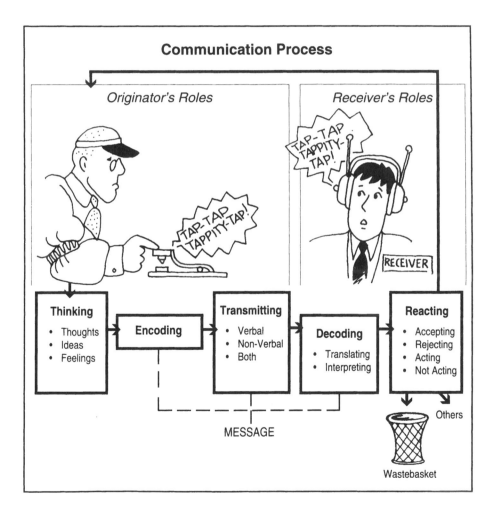

A good deal of business writing quite appropriately adopts an impersonal, neutral tone. But sometimes that tone is hard to come by when you need it: when you're angry or apologetic or required to be the bearer of bad tidings. Then you need techniques to recover your poise. And sometimes you're neutral and impersonal out of mere bad habit. Sometimes you can well afford to lighten up and make your correspondence stand out in the gray and beige world by giving it the brighter colors of your own signature, leaving your own imprint, even using some well-placed humor.

AVOIDING THE NEGATIVE BY ACCENTUATING THE POSITIVE

- Use antonyms to remove the obviously negative "not."

Instead of	*Write*
He did not accept the help.	He declined the help.
The office will not be open then.	The office will be closed then.
They were not present during the conference call.	They were absent during the conference call.
The meeting did not start on time.	The meeting started late.

- Use synonyms to avoid wordy, negative-sounding phrases.

Instead of	*Write*
not acceptable	unsuitable, unfit
not important	minor
does not like	prefers
did not pay heed to	avoided
did not have much faith in	doubted

- Soften with the passive voice.

Instead of	*Write*
You did not enclose payment.	Payment was not enclosed.
You did not submit your form before the penalty period.	Your form was not mailed before the penalty period.
You have made three errors in your report.	Three errors were found in the report.

- Be alert to shades of meaning that your words carry. Distinguish the useful from the awful. When you can't be positive, use neutral language to sound more factual.

Negative	*Neutral*	*Positive*
corporate dictate	company policy	company belief
obvious	clear, plain	notable
confrontation	discussion	meeting
deep doo-doo	predicament	opportunity
getup	dress/apparel	ensemble
calculating/shrewd/ cunning	clever/bright	astute
come clean/confess	acknowledge	grant
intimidate	startle	overawe
roly-poly	heavyset	substantial
pigsty	house/residence/ apartment	mansion/home
demolished	broke up	sacrificed
beat	master	excel
featherweight	inexperienced	fresh
defiant	independent	self-reliant, autonomous
battle-ax	quarrelsome	strong willed
infamous	well-known	famous
foreign	non-native	international

- Remember your reader is a human being. Refrain from writing like a bossy parent chiding a child. Treat your reader like an adult.

Defensive Climates	*Supportive Climates*
Readers tend to become defensive toward people who seem to be	Readers tend to communicate openly with people who seem to be
<ul><li>evaluating their behavior</li><li>trying to control them</li><li>trying to manipulate them</li><li>indifferent to their welfare</li><li>considering themselves superior</li><li>knowing it all</li></ul>	<ul><li>describing their behavior</li><li>cooperating in solving a problem</li><li>acting spontaneously</li><li>concerned with their welfare</li><li>considering themselves equal</li><li>open to others' ideas</li></ul>

Adapted from J. R. Gibb's "Defensive Communication," *Journal of Communication*, vol. XI, no. 3 (September 1961): 141–48.

DELIVERING UNPOPULAR MESSAGES

When you deal with the most difficult writing situations—apologizing, reprimanding, giving bad news—you can use these guidelines.

Lowering the Hot Water's Temperature

Do	*Don't*
■ Do state your purpose up front.	Don't start with once-upon-a-time detail.
■ Do opt for neutral words when you can't be positive, and be courteous (though not patronizing even when you have the authority to command).	Don't use hostile, inflammatory words that make your reader see red (failed, refused, must, should, imperative, etc.) or words with strong negative connotations.
■ Do allow your reader to save face. That is, minimize attack on the person. Focus on the issue. For example, "An out-of-stock condition has developed" is preferable to "You've created a problem." (That's using the passive voice to your advantage.)	Don't "scream" in print. This includes using sarcasm, unless you aim it at yourself.
■ Do focus on what you have done and what the reader can do to resolve the problem. If possible, give the reader a choice. State what actions you've taken to remedy the situation.	Don't belabor your assault. (Also, don't cry all over the memo with overblown apologies if you are at fault.)
■ Do inject people's names and use contractions to warm your writing and to sound natural.	Don't be stuffy, inflated, or adorned even when bearing bad news.
■ Do be consistent in your tone (i.e., formal/informal throughout).	Don't confuse your reader by playing the chameleon in your memo. Your reader will find your mixed tones, at best, confusing; at worst, insincere.

EXAMINING TONE

If thought corrupts language, language can also corrupt thought.
George Orwell

Some memos make readers defensive: Too much in them "sounds" wrong. Some memos sit better with you. Read the following four examples, monitor your reactions, and identify the tone of each one at the top of the page. Then identify the words and phrases most responsible for creating that tone.

Memo #1 First Draft

FROM:	R.N.I. Harsh, Managing Partner
TO:	Davidson & Associates Consultants
CC:	
BCC:	
SUBJECT:	Request for Delinquent Materials: Third Request

MATERIAL REQUIRED: All pertinent materials

FOR PERIOD: From June 30 to September 29 – Work must be here by November 1 or sooner.

THESE RECORDS ARE OVERDUE.

We cannot overemphasize the need for you to comply with the work program we have designed for you. Your failure to meet the requirements of this program creates problems in our internal work procedures. Further, you are creating penalty situations that can be avoided by adhering to the work schedule.

Your immediate response will be appreciated. Should you have any comments relative to the above, do not hesitate to call.

Memo #1 Revision

FROM:	R.N.I. (Les) Harsh, Managing Partner
TO:	Davidson & Associates Consultants
CC:	
BCC:	
SUBJECT:	Third Quarter Records Needed to Avoid Additional Payments

To prepare your third-quarter reports before the November 1 deadline, I need your income and expense records from June 30 to September 29. Any further delays at this already late date will result in costly penalties.

What's needed now is your quick response. Please send me your records by overnight priority mail.

That way, you, I, and the Office of Taxation will be aligned.

Memo #2 First Draft

Memorandum

TO: Word-Processing Staff

FROM: Ben. T. Outashape

SUBJECT: A New Beginning

There are some activities that have been permitted in this department in the past that are unacceptable. This is my fourth week with the department and I have had an opportunity to observe that the following activities are daily occurrences and not isolated incidences. The purpose of this memo is to provide all employees in this department with a clear understanding of what is expected by the company and myself from 8:15 to 4:30 on a daily basis. You are here because your services are needed in whatever position you are working.

We begin the *working day* at 8:15; for that reason you need to be at your desk at 8:15 ready to begin work. If you arrive prior to that time and are not working overtime, take care of visiting with coworkers (those who are also not working) and any other needs you may have that are not work related. You have all seen the memo from Sara Buckley concerning food at the desk; if you have not I will provide you with a copy. This means at 8:15 we do not peel apples, oranges, grapefruit, or anything else. We go to work. Current lunch hour is from 11:30 to 12:15. Let's work until 11:30 and return to our desk promptly at 12:15 and resume work for the afternoon. Production reports are not to be prepared before 4:15, after which you may clear off your desk to leave at 4:30. Since I have been with this department, I have seen occasions when cleanup began at 3:45 by some, no all, employees—NO MORE!! Remain at your desk until departure time (4:30), and then leave quietly. Please have some consideration for your fellow employees who are still working. This is a business office and we should maintain that atmosphere.

Memo #2 First Draft (continued)

(2)

Personal telephone calls need to be limited. If you have friends who call you at work just to chat or if you have been in the habit of calling them during working hours for social reasons, give them notice. They can call you at home. This is a business telephone. We recognize there are times when you have emergencies or need to speak with your spouse, children, doctor's office, and other business offices whose hours are the same as those at this office. We make allowances for these needs. Some of these can be handled during your lunch hour, and since others in the department may have the same needs, keep it brief.

Visiting with friends or relatives in other departments during working hours is also not allowed. This disrupts the work of the employees you may be talking with and may create problems for that employee as well as yourself.

Any continuation of the above-mentioned practices will be addressed on an individual basis. The purpose of addressing these problems in memo form is to provide each employee in this department with a clear understanding in written form of what the expectations are from a work standpoint. If you have any questions or concerns, I will be available to discuss them with you individually. I will retain a copy of this memo for each of you. It will serve as a document to mark a beginning point for any further discussion that may be necessary on these issues. I urge you to give this some serious consideration.

Memo #2 Revision

TO: Word-Processing Staff

FROM: Ben T. Outashape

SUBJECT: Rules of the Road: Important Reminders About Department
           Practices and Policies

Since I joined this department as manager, I've been able to observe how
we function—and how we don't. These reminders about department policy
are in order.

Workday   • The workday begins at 8:15. That means that
Schedule   everyone should be ready to start working at 8:15, not
                    getting ready to work at 8:30 or 8:45.

                  • Lunch break begins at 11:30 and ends at 12:15.

                  • The workday ends at 4:30. At 4:15, not 3:45, the
                    end-of-day routine begins. Prepare your production
                    report, clean up your desk, and quietly leave the office
                    at 4:30. Be considerate of your colleagues who are still
                    working.

Phone Calls   • Our phones should be reserved primarily for business
                    purposes.
                    - When you need to use the telephone to contact your
                      spouse or children, or to make appointments, keep
                      your conversations brief.
                    - Whenever possible, make such calls during your
                      lunch break.
                    - Discourage friends from calling you to chat by
                      suggesting that they call you at home instead.

Visiting at   • Catch up with your coworkers before 8:15, during
the Office   lunch, or after 4:30. Keep the working day for work.
                    All of us work more accurately and productively when
                    undistracted.

Housekeeping • Sara Buckley, VP HR, has sent all of us a reminder
                    that we work at our desk and eat at the tables in the
                    lounge. Apple cores, orange peels, grapefruit sections,
                    and other edibles have been migrating from the
                    lounge to the office. Let's keep them where they
                    belong.

These guidelines can be summed up in a general rule: This is a business
office, and we should behave accordingly.

If you'd like clarification of any of these points, let me know. I'm eager to
help all of us meet the company's expectations for professional behavior.

Now you try to revise. Keep in mind that you want your reader to respond supportively, not defensively, to your advice. And use more tact, please.

Toning Exercise

SUBJECT: Poor Team Effort

In some cases I feel there is a lack of togetherness in the organizations. Everyone must work together toward a common goal. Your employees should be expected to take part in all promotions and incentive programs. It is their responsibility to sell, deliver, and merchandise our products. It is your responsibility to see that they have the proper equipment to work with and that the equipment is properly maintained. You should provide rewards that encourage your employees to exert that second effort. You should see that morale is high and that all employees take pride in their job and in their employer.

<u>MINIMUM EFFORTS WILL NOT WORK!!!</u>

Best regards,

U. Gettit

Here's a revised version to compare with yours.

Toning-Exercise Revision

SUBJECT: Team Effort Guarantees Success

Our success in a crowded marketplace depends in part on the individual efforts of those who sell, deliver, and merchandise our products. But it depends in far larger part on our coordinated efforts. One of your most important tasks as a manager is to make it possible for your employees to work together toward their common goal.

Here are a few ways to carry out that crucial task:

- Encourage your employees to participate in all promotions and incentive programs.

- Provide your employees with the equipment they need to do their work.

- Maintain the equipment.

- Provide rewards that encourage your employees to make that second effort.

- Keep morale high.

- Encourage pride in the job and the company.

You have a challenging job and the company's full confidence that you can perform it well. Let me know how I can support your efforts.

USING HUMOR

Laughter is the shortest distance between two people.
Victor Borge

The key to achieving a tone that works? When you write, anticipate your reader's likely response, and ward off common negative responses such as anger, unhappiness, suspicion, and indifference by acknowledging your reader's feelings and/or emphasizing what's in it for the reader. Novel approaches and, yes, humor can sometimes help.

Will Rogers quipped, "An onion can make people cry, but there has never been a vegetable invented to make them laugh." Nor a piece of business correspondence, I might add.

While humor has been used successfully in business meetings, conferences, and negotiations, very little has found its way into our corporate correspondence. And it's time it did.

"Sacrilege," you say. "Business writing," you contend, "is no laughing matter."

Agreed. Sort of. Writing in the workplace *is* serious business. But that doesn't mean it has to be solemn. Yet too much is.

In workplace writing, many people assume a persona, don a dour attitude, and avoid using humor, thinking they may not be taken seriously otherwise. And through such thinking and writing, they miss a handful (and ha-ha-ful) of opportunities to accomplish their job more easily, more humanly.

Even history supports the value of humor: Many of our most respected leaders have used their sense of humor to motivate, stimulate, surprise, dissolve tension, awaken their audiences to action—and acceptance. And brain research confirms the biological and psychological value of laughter, which releases endorphins, the body's own pain-reducing substance. Additional research has claimed a correlation between a well-developed sense of humor and problem solving. And yet, flat, blah business prose persists, in large part because people are intimidated by the business world, insecure in it, and restrained by narrow notions about what is professional.

All this ballyhoo about sounding professional on paper has resulted in ballyhumdrum: boring, pompous, stiff writing. Puritan prose, mealy memos, regurgitated reports. Mechanically correct (maybe) but devoid of human breath or life. Perhaps in the past, writers could get away with boring, formulaic, and pretentious letters and memos. Today, however, the sheer volume of correspondence dictates that our writing be fresh and vital. Humor and a light touch can give your writing that extra edge.

Humor *can* make a memo more memorable. I am not saying that humor is the antidote (or anecdote!) for every situation, but it does have a legitimate, even desirable position in business writing. Appropriate humor need not remain a subversive, out-of-place activity in the workplace.

Of course, use common sense along with your comic sense. Being light yet serious is not without risk. One person's pun may be another's poison. Think about your audience and what you want your writing to accomplish. Do you know your audience? It's difficult—and dangerous—to try a light touch with strangers. Have previous straightforward attempts failed to get something done? Has your present style produced your hoped-for results? Are you (and your readers) bored with your stiff stuffiness? If so, a humorous approach is a risk worth taking.

Naturally, some humor ought to be avoided. Sarcasm and sexual and ethnic references have no place in either writing or speech. Neither does insulting, acid humor; laughing with, not at, your supervisor or coworkers is a wiser career move. As with irreverent humor, also forgo the irrelevant. And don't overload with humor—use just enough to captivate your reader and humanize yourself. Contrary to popular messages about "being professional," your authority won't waver—and your likability will leap.

Admittedly, it's easier to pull off a light touch face-to-face in a business situation. After all, you have tone of voice, inflection, and body language to help your audience understand your intent. And you are present to change your approach if you see it isn't working. In writing, you are absent when your audience reads your words and, as a result, more prone to be misunderstood. Yes, writing is inherently more difficult. So if you are uncomfortable trying for humor in your writing, let's compromise: At least be neutral, not stilted. It *is* possible to take the stiffness out while keeping the professionalism in.

When there's opportunity—and willingness—to take a risk, opt for the humorous, not the tumorous or timorous touch.

Exactly what serious work can a light touch help you accomplish? Plenty. Let me share some examples.

- **A humorous memo nourishes: It helps motivate/involve colleagues; it builds camaraderie, heightens morale.**

Memo #1

DATE: June 7
TO: New Products
FROM: Eileen Brown
SUBJECT: New Products Group Outing
      (or, "You will have team spirit, or else!")

It's time once again to honor that venerable tradition, the New Products Group Outing. (Or, time to make fools of ourselves in front of our coworkers and create material for our going-away roasts.)

This is a mandatory survey: If you do not return your copy in a timely manner, the responsibility for planning this event will automatically pass to you!

FIRST, WHAT DO YOU WANT TO DO?

Rank the following activities in order of preference (1 is what you live for, 2 is a pretty-good idea, 3 is you can take it or leave it, 4 means you'd rather be in the office working, and 5 means if we pick this, you *will* be in the office working):

White-water rafting   _____
Canoeing   _____
War games   _____
Beach party   _____
Mets or Yanks   _____

_____   _____
(Write-in ballot)

Remember, none of these is free!

Memo #1 (continued)

SECOND, WHEN DO YOU WANT TO DO IT?

All of these activities are one-day ideas. In order to keep us fresh and well rested for Monday, I've listed a few possible Saturdays we can party (because on the seventh day even New Products has to rest).

Pay attention now! For this question, place an *X* next to the days you would be available to have fun. Leave blank those days you are planning to stay home and be miserable.

July 15	_____	August 7	_____
July 23	_____	August 13	_____
July 30	_____	August 20	_____
		August 27	_____

THIRD, WHOM DO YOU WANT TO BRING?

No, this is not where we rank our preference for members of the department. This is where you reveal your deepest, darkest secret—do you *really* like your children?

Keeping in mind that we have to pay for all this fun, you can now decide just how important your significant other and/or kiddies are to you. (If you are really nice to me, I promise not to show your spouse/friend/children your answers to this question.)

Yet another type of question (for all the ex-marketing researchers in the group)! Place an *X* next to the *one* statement that you agree with most:

1. It is not possible to have fun with my significant other and /or kids; therefore, I think we should all come alone.   _____

2. I am lost without my significant other and will definitely bring her/him. However, the kids will bother everyone if they come.   _____

3. I aspire to be like Bill Cosby; therefore, my entire family and assorted pets will accompany me for good, wholesome family fun.   _____

Thank you for your prompt response (by Friday).

In Memo #1, the organizer of the company outing took her job seriously, yet lightheartedly. By letting her creativity reign, she had fun with her task and, in doing so, showed her coworkers she cared about them, about getting their attention and their input. And she came across as no less a professional in the process.

■ **A novel approach to a problem reduces defensiveness/invites an audience to laugh at counterproductive behavior.**

Memo #2

FROM:	Steve Davidson
TO:	Sales Managers
CC:	
BCC:	
SUBJECT:	Monthly Reports

Once upon a time there was a farmer who owned a mule. He sold the mule to his neighbor with the stipulation that the mule had to be treated kindly and spoken to softly, or it would not work. The neighbor took the mule home. The next day when he went to the barn to get the mule so he could do some plowing, he could not get the mule out of the barn. He treated the mule kindly and spoke to it softly, all to no avail. The mule refused to move.

He called the farmer and told him of his plight. The farmer immediately came to the neighbor's farm and took a big 2x4 out of his pickup truck, walked into the barn and hit the mule square between the eyes. The neighbor became quite upset. He said, "What are you doing? You told me I had to treat this mule kindly."

The farmer replied, "You do—but first you have to get his attention."

We now have a 2x4 in the district office. As of January, those sales managers who are *still* sending monthly reports in late, and those sales managers who are not sending them in at all, will be summoned to the district office so that we can get your attention.

When previous memos about overdue or missing reports have had no effect, perhaps it's time to reprimand in a refreshing, yet powerful way. Traditional reprimands, usually those beginning with "It has come to my attention that" merely shuffle paper from one desk to the next without resolving anything. In fact, they often alienate employees, further fueling the problem.

In the 2×4 memo, the guilty can see a manager who has taken the time to be novel in approaching an issue and who appears more human than the manager who writes, "This action must cease and desist immediately." Human nature being what it is, most of us prefer being chastised in a way that doesn't strip away our dignity. A wholesome, humorous approach allows that.

■ **Humor can turn a negative situation into a positive one, defuse anger, and quell skepticism.**

This approach, illustrated in the following e-mails, appeased employees who wanted to stay angry at the company and criticize it as inept after a computer error caused pink slips to be included in everyone's paycheck.

Memo #3

FROM:	N. Brunetti
TO:	All Employees
CC:	
BCC:	
SUBJECT:	Pink-Slip Glitch

June 16

Oops . . . to err is human; to really foul things up takes a computer.

If you received a termination notice in your pay envelope, don't panic. Our computer decided it could operate the facilities by itself. It has since been counseled and should not attempt another unfriendly takeover.

See you in the morning, and bring your pink slip to the cafeteria. Breakfast is on us!

Or here's another version.

Received a pink slip? Not to worry. The computer printed one for itself as well.

Disregard the termination notice. The paycheck, however, is real. Sorry for the glitch . . . computers are people, too.

- **Humor minimizes resistance and deflects criticism.**

Here's a manager who knows his staff and anticipates/acknowledges their gut reaction to having to complete an involved task without adequate lead time. In acknowledging their negative feelings, he defuses them. They did the work and appreciated the memo.

Memo #4
- **Humor gets read because it's different from businessese.**

DATE:	April 12
TO:	Distribution
FROM	Eric Davis
SUBJECT:	Completing Hayy Compensation Survey

I've enclosed the data-input package for the Hayy compensation survey. You will notice that we have little lead time for divisions to complete the information. (I have purchased two flak jackets and steel helmets for Dorothy and me, so comment as you will.)

Bob Davis has assured me that both he and Joan Murphy will be available to assist with questions that need to be answered at the last minute. I'm sure that you've noticed from the due date it *is* the last minute.

I will also be available (if I can be found). Please call me if you need help. If you would like to vent your frustrations, please call Dorothy.

Be it to compliment or complain, humor is a valuable tool to make your point.

Memo #5

5 Exasperated Way
New Bedford, MA 02740

June 4

Executive Office Supplies
Accounts Payable
1010 Arlington Blvd.
Outtogetcha, VT 00000

Dear Computer:

Writing to you directly seems the last action left for me to get my account (#0875342) properly credited. My two previous attempts have somehow gotten lost in your memory bank. Let me retrace our stormy relationship:

STEP	DATE	ACTION
1.	April 1	You write stating that I owe $972 on my account.
2.	April 4	I respond in writing (copy attached) reporting that a check (#2851) for the full amount was sent on March 15, the day the invoice was received.
3.	May 1	Repeat of Step 1. Letter sounds more urgent.
4.	May 4	I respond in writing (copy attached) and enclose a copy of the cancelled check, verifying the payment in question.
5.	June 1	Repeat of Step 1. This time the letter sounds downright ornery.
6.	June 4	I am now appealing to you directly, having been unsuccessful with Steps 2 and 4. Once again, I enclose a copy of the cancelled check.

Clearly, I have done all necessary to confirm that my account balance is zero.

Will you—or your operator—finally debug my account and remove me from your list of Bad Guys?

Sincerely,
Esther Falk

enclosures

Sometimes it takes only an attention-getting opening, as in

> "Our prayers have been answered. Our plea has been heard. We received the additional sales promotional items we requested."

> or

> "I've got egg on my face and need your help."

Such openings are honest and natural, and get attention because they are.

■ **Humor can help you get the first draft written—in that draft you can safely vent.**

Write anything down for that first draft. It doesn't have to be right the first time. Just say it any way, even if it's sarcastic. Then look it over, remove the inappropriate tone, neutralize. The usefulness of a first, funny draft is that it helps you cope with the situation.

If you remove the deadpan delivery from your correspondence, if you take yourself a bit less seriously, you'll raise not just a smile or a laugh but also your own success quotient.

How to Infuse Your Writing with Humor

1. Be yourself. Take a risk. But use common sense along with your comic sense.

2. Use analogies to make your point more concrete and understandable.

3. Create a sense of connectedness to your audience by referring to an aspect in the workplace that is universally known, admired, frowned at, poked fun of. In short, tap the workplace culture.

4. Use unusual, but not snooty, words or phrases.

5. Play with language and with word order to create an unusual, original effect.

6. Include yourself in the humor.

7. If writing to subordinates, make a playful, not an egotistical, show of authority.

8. Take advantage of opportunities to be relaxed and playful. Announcements, farewells, transmittals, and internal memos to audiences you know present a place to start.

Humor Exercise

Go back to your revision of the team-effort memo (page 155) and try a humorous approach to the situation. Then compare yours to the two that follow.

SUBJECT: It Takes Team Effort

John Heisman, explaining what a football was on the first day of practice, said: "A prolate spheroid—that is, an elongated sphere—in which the outer leathern casing is drawn tightly over a somewhat smaller rubber tubing . . . better to have died a small boy than to fumble this."

In much the same way, better not to fumble our success in today's crowded marketplace. In part, completing a successful pass depends on the individual efforts of those who sell, deliver, and merchandise our products. But it depends in far larger part on our coordinated efforts.

Here are a few ways to carry out that crucial task:

• En
  pro

• Pro

• Ma

• Pro

• Ke

• En

You

SUBJECT: No More Monday-Morning Quarterback

Each fall, football coaches react to the critics much as you probably do when you read a "motivational" memo from me: "If you really want to give me advice," they say, "do it on Saturday afternoon between one and four o'clock, when you've got 25 seconds to do it, between plays. Don't give me advice on Monday. I know the right thing to do on Monday."

The time is now Saturday afternoon, and we're in the midst of a crowded marketplace. Our success there depends in part on the individual efforts of those who sell, deliver, and merchandise our products. But it depends in far larger part on our coordinated efforts. One of your most important tasks as a manager is to make it possible for your employees to work together toward their common goal.

Here are a few ways to carry out that crucial task:
• Encourage your employees to participate in all promotions and incentive programs.
• Provide your employees with the equipment they need to do their work.
• Maintain the equipment.
• Provide rewards that encourage your employees to make that second effort.
• Keep morale high.
• Encourage pride in the job and the company.

You have a challenging job and the company's full confidence that you can perform it well. Let me know how I can support your efforts.

If a sports analogy won't dovetail with your business/profession, choose an analogy that your readers can identify with. As is evident from these examples, to achieve a lighthearted tone with a serious intent, you needn't riddle your writing with comedic effect. A little well-placed humor will work.

BANISHING BIAS

The emotional, sexual, and psychological stereotyping of females begins when the doctor says "It's a girl."

—former Congresswoman Shirley Chisholm

Through the years, changes have worked their way into our writing and speech. Today people are more conscious about using language that unintentionally implies bias toward gender, age, race, or ability.

To avoid raised eyebrows, examine your writing carefully. Know your audience and their sensitivities. Then use words and phrases that offer equal treatment and eliminate bias. In short, avoid mentioning gender, age, race, or ability unless it is pertinent to your message.

Gender Bias

Biased	*Alternative*
adman	ad executive, account executive
airman	flier, pilot, aviator
anchorman	anchor
bellboy	bellhop
the best man for the job	the best person for the job
businessman	professional, business manager, executive
chairman	chair, coordinator, head
common man	common person
fireman	fire fighter
fisherman	angler
foreman	supervisor
freshman	first-year student
mailman	mail carrier
man-hours	hours, time, labor

Biased	*Alternative*
mankind	humanity, people, human beings
man-made	synthetic, manufactured
manpower	personnel, human resources, staff
men working	roadwork
my girl	my secretary, my assistant
policeman	police officer
salesman	sales representative, salesperson
spokesman	spokesperson
stewardess	flight attendant
waiter, waitress	wait staff, server
workman	worker

"Let's try again. If you stop calling me 'Honey,'
I won't address you as 'Poopsie Pie.'"

To eliminate gender, age, race, and ability bias, rewrite in the plural, reword, or replace the masculine pronoun with *one, you,* or (sparingly) *he* or *she*, as appropriate.

Not This	*But This*
■ Give each employee his notice as soon as he returns from lunch.	Give the employees their notice as soon as they return from lunch.
■ A competent manager solicits feedback about his performance.	A competent manager solicits feed back about performance.
■ If the quality-control supervisor is dissatisfied with the output, he may shut down production.	A quality-control supervisor dissatisfied with the output may shut down production.
	or
	As a quality control supervisor, if you are dissatisfied with the output, you may shut down production.
■ Everyone should send in his/her report.	Everyone should submit a report.
	or
	All employees should submit their report.
■ Each employee should complete his assessment.	Each employee should complete an assessment.
	or
	All employees should complete their assessment.
■ If he works hard, a district manager can expect promotion.	If they work hard, district managers can expect promotion.
■ An employee can contact his claims representative.	You can contact your claims representative.
	or
	Employees can contact their claims representative.

Not This	_But This_
■ Each candidate must complete his letter of intent.	Each candidate must complete a letter of intent.
■ The employee is hired after he shows . . .	The employee is hired after showing . . .
■ On Tuesdays, senior citizens will receive a 10 percent discount on purchases.	On Tuesdays, anyone over 55 will receive a 10 percent discount on purchases.
■ Students from culturally disadvantaged backgrounds . . .	Students from homes where English is not spoken . . .
	_or_
	Students from homes where reading has not been stressed . . .
■ The course appealed to nonwhite students.	The course appealed to students of all racial backgrounds.
■ A disabled student rang the alarm.	A student rang the alarm.
■ A deaf worker taught her department how to sign.	A worker who is deaf taught her department how to sign.
■ A handicapped employee requested the ramp be repaired.	An employee who uses a wheelchair requested the ramp be repaired.

Politically correct (PC) language, in an effort to keep from sounding biased, usually ends up sounding like euphemese. Use with care!

Would you prefer being old . . .   or chronologically gifted?

Is he stupid . . .   or just differently logical?

Is he nearsighted . . .   or just optically inconvenienced?

Do you know someone motivationally deficient (i.e., lazy)?
Or non-traditionally ordered (i.e., disorganized)?

Part 5 Getting It Right: The Basics of Grammar and Spelling

. . . here and there a touch of good grammar for picturesqueness.

Mark Twain

11
Grappling with Grammar

Executives who feel badly about not writing good, irregardless of their education or position, will find it helpful to look farther into this section.

And anyone who thinks the above sentence reads correctly definitely ought to continue reading! "Feel badly," "good versus well," and "irregardless" are among the top grammatical/usage errors in written—and spoken—business communication. These mistakes are made by assistants and managers alike—hurting their personal image as well as the company's.

If you speak and write for your company, your words *do* matter. It pays to make them the right ones. Toward that end, this section answers the questions asked most often by business professionals about grammar, usage, and sentence mechanics. And it provides solutions to your biggest/most frequent mistakes as well.

The administrative assistant called the board members names.

THE SEVEN DEADLY SINS OF GRAMMAR

Question: What are the most frequent mistakes made—
or what are the seven deadly sins?

1. INCORRECT PRONOUNS

- **Using the pronoun *myself* incorrectly.**

    Incorrect: They shipped the order to Tom and myself.

    Incorrect: Debra and myself headed the committee.

    Why are these wrong? The reflexive pronoun "-self" is not interchangeable with "I" or "me." It's correct when used for emphasis, as in

    > The President himself makes grammar goofs.
    > I myself have to think about the rules.

    It's also correct when used as a reflexive pronoun—that is, when it refers to a noun or pronoun used earlier.

    > RULE: You need a reflexive pronoun when the subject and the object of the action are the same.

    We wouldn't say "I fly me to seminars."

    I fly myself to seminars.

    She gave herself a raise.

    "She gave her a raise" means something else entirely. Thus

    Correct: They shipped the order to Tom and me.

    Correct: Debra and I headed the committee.

    Which brings us to the next most common error in grammar.

- **Using *I* for *me*.**

    Incorrect: Send your invoices to Luis or I.

    (We would never say "Send your invoices to I.")

    Incorrect: This decision will be made between you and I.

> RULE: *I* is always the subject of a verb.

Correct: Debra and I headed the committee.
I is the subject; *me* is always the object of a verb or preposition.

Correct: They shipped the order to Tom and me.

Me is the object of the preposition *to*.

Correct: Send your invoices to Luis or me.

Me is the object of the preposition *to*.

Correct: This decision will be made between you and me.

Me is the object of the preposition *between*.

- **Switching from singular to plural pronoun reference.**

> RULE: Pronouns need to agree in number and gender with the nouns to which they refer.

Incorrect: *Each* employee must punch *their* time card before leaving.

Correct: Each employee must punch a time card before leaving.

or

All employees must punch their time card before leaving.

Incorrect: *Each* division manager will address *their* wholesalers at the convention.

Correct: *All* division managers will address *their* wholesalers at the conference.

(Switching to the plural is preferable to risking the biased "Each division manager will address his wholesalers at the conference," or the awkward "Each will address his or her wholesalers.")

2. SUBJECT-VERB DISAGREEMENT

This can occur when there's an intervening phrase between subject and verb.

Incorrect: The boxes containing the missing information is being delivered Friday.

Incorrect: Each of the managers agree with the decision.

Incorrect: The consensus of past conference attendees were positive.

Incorrect: Multiple production environments, although offering business flexibility, has caused us to endure increased completely.

Other rules apply for subject-verb agreement, but this is the one that causes the most errors.

3. LACK OF PARALLEL STRUCTURE

Writing related parts of a sentence, heading, or list in similar grammatical form makes reading easier. You set up an expectation for your reader, and when you abandon your pattern, you create confusion.

Unparallel: I see one third of a nation ill housed, ill clothed, and not getting any food.

Parallel: I see one third of a nation ill housed, ill clothed, ill nourished.

Unparallel: Anita requested we (1) define our mission statement; (2) set up individual objectives; (3) determining budgets; and (4) the approval process begins.

Parallel: Anita requested we (1) define our mission statement; (2) set up individual objectives; (3) determine budgets; and (4) begin the approval process.

Unparallel: Dorothy Carin was happy about her promotion and getting a pay raise.

Parallel: Dorothy Carin was happy about her promotion and pay raise.

Unparallel: The sales manager advises employees to work hard and against relying on luck.

Parallel: The sales manager advises employees to work hard and not to rely on luck.

Unparallel: The service center promises to sell us the truck parts and that the cost will be reasonable.

Parallel: The service center promises to sell us the truck parts and to keep the cost reasonable.

Also, when you bullet or number points, remember to maintain parallelism.

Before Parallelism

1. A new computer
2. Repair disk drive
3. Readjust overtime rates
4. Reviewing job descriptions

After Parallelism

1. Purchase new computer
2. Repair disk drive
3. Readjust overtime rates
4. Review job descriptions

Memo Before Parallelism

DATE: 9/3
TO: T. Samuels
FROM: B. Frugle
SUBJECT: Expense Control

This correspondence confirms the necessary action to be taken in regard to expense control, which we discussed extensively on 9/1.

1. Air travel will be eliminated unless extremely advantageous and at bargain fares.
2. Lodging, to be limited, except where absolutely required—and then moderately priced accommodations will be sought.
3. Immediately investigate long-distance telephone savings possible.
4. Gasoline prices will be monitored and savings obtained.
5. Attempt will be made to reduce entertainment—judiciously.

Memo After Parallelism

DATE: 9/3
TO: T. Samuels
FROM: B. Frugle
SUBJECT: Confirming Expense Control Plan

These are the steps we agreed to take to reduce expenses by 20 percent over the next quarter.

1. Eliminate air travel unless advantageous and at bargain fares.
2. Limit lodging except where absolutely required—and then seek moderately priced accommodations.
3. Investigate long-distance telephone savings possible.
4. Monitor gasoline prices and obtain savings.
5. Reduce entertainment—judiciously.

Thanks for helping put together this action plan. I'm looking forward to seeing our savings.

4. RUN-ON SENTENCES WITH THE WORD *HOWEVER*

Many business writers wrongly join two independent clauses with *however* or its first cousins *moreover, therefore, nevertheless*, and *furthermore*. These adverbial conjunctions lack the power of *and, but, or,* or *nor*. That is, they *cannot* join two independent clauses with only a comma. To solve this dilemma, rewrite run-ons as separate sentences, join them with a semi-colon, or revise the sentence.

Run-on: I agree with you, however, I plan to avoid putting my opinion in writing.

Correct: I agree with you; however, I plan to avoid putting my opinion in writing.

or

I agree with you. I plan, however, to avoid putting my opinion in writing.

(A semicolon after *you* would also work.)

or

While I agree with you, I plan to avoid putting my opinion in writing.

Run-on: Our promotion was successful, however the competition also lowered its discount prices.

Correct: Our promotion was successful; however, the competition also lowered its prices.

or

Our promotion was successful. The competition, however, also lowered its prices.

or

Our promotion was successful, but the competition had also lowered its prices.

5. DANGLING PHRASES, UNCLEAR REFERENCES, AND MISPLACED MODIFIERS
These are errors of placement.

■ **Dangling Phrases**

Dangling: Checking the computer room, the dog was found.

Correct: Checking the computer room, security found the dog.

Problem: Dangling phrases usually begin a sentence. What they modify is omitted.

■ **Unclear References**

Unclear: Having been told that he was incompetent and dishonest, the executive fired the man.

Who was called incompetent and dishonest? The executive? The man?

Correct: Having told the man that he was incompetent and dishonest, the executive fired him.

or

Having called his superior incompetent and dishonest, the man was fired.

Unclear: According to the sales rep's report, the truck apparently ran off Busch Road and struck the traffic light as it attempted to get back on the roadway.

Correct: According to the sales rep's report, as the truck was attempting to get back on the roadway, it apparently ran off Busch Road and struck the traffic light.

Unclear: Do not park your delivery truck at the taxi stand or it will be towed away.

Correct: If you park at the taxi stand, your truck will be towed.

Unclear: The supervisor informed the customer that they will match the competitor's price if he can provide a quote.

Correct: The supervisor informed the customer that if the customer can provide a quote, the company will match the competitor's price.

Unclear: Joe e-mailed the report to Tom just before he left for vacation.

Correct: Just before Joe left for vacation, he e-mailed the report to Tom.

▪ Misplaced Modifiers

Watch *all* the modifiers in a sentence. Each needs to be neatly placed near or next to what it is modifying. Otherwise, the results may be, at best, laughable; at worst, costly.

Misplaced: Here are some suggestions for handling obscene complaint calls from corporate headquarters.

Correct: Corporate headquarters offers the following suggestions for handling obscene phone calls.

Misplaced: The district managers discussed the high cost of living with two women sales reps.

Correct: The district manager discussed with two sales reps the high cost of living.

Misplaced: The beautiful display at the event was donated in memory of Mr. Ben Gone who was accidentally killed last year by his wife, children, and grandchildren.

Correct: The beautiful display at the event was donated by the wife, children, and grandchildren of Mr. Ben Gone, who died accidentally last year.

RULE: Place your modifiers close to the words they modify.

Misplaced: The sales rep placed the promotional merchandise in the van that he had just received from the company.

Correct: The sales rep placed the promotional merchandise that he had just received from the company in the van.

Misplaced: I have discussed how to fill the empty containers with my employees.

Correct: I have discussed with my employees how to fill the empty containers.

I have discussed how to fill the empty containers with my employees.

Misplaced: Proposal to employ retirees not yet dead.
Correct: Proposal still alive to employ retirees.

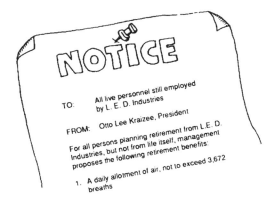

Here are some more laughable examples from syndicated columnist James Kilpatrick.

From Ohio Senator John Glenn, announcing hearings on alcohol abuse:
One proposal would revoke the license "of any driver found to be intoxicated for a period of 90 days."

From a Trenton, NJ, paper, interviewing a lottery winner:
"He visits the Queens, New York, cemetery where Houdini is buried twice each year."

From a Washington, D.C., paper, reviewing a community-development program:
"While only six years old, members of the county planning commission have admitted it is time to update the community plan."

From *Running Times*, publishing an item on a female long-distance runner:
"Six months pregnant, her doctor told her she could run through July."

From a Buffalo, NY, paper, warning:
"The Health Department has been urging people not to eat raw clams or clams that have not been cooked for years."

6. CONFUSING WORD PAIRS

*The difference between the right word and the almost right word
is the difference between "lightning" and "lightning bug."*
Mark Twain

Certain word pairs haunt writers. Among/between the words that most often perplex, you'll find these:

affect	v.	effect		
anxious	v.	eager		
beside	v.	besides		
bring	v.	take		
can	v.	may		
fewer	v.	less		
its	v.	it's		
pseudo-	v.	quasi-		
than	v.	then		
their	v.	there	v.	they're

Commonly Confused Word Pairs and Homonyms

A

abrogate . . . . abolish
abdicate . . . .abandon

accede . . . . .agree
exceed . . . .surpass

accept . . . . . .*verb,* to receive
except . . . . . .*preposition,* excluding, omitting

access . . . . . .admittance
excess. . . . . . too much

addition . . . .increase
edition. . . . . published form

advice . . . . . .*noun,* recommendation
advise . . . . . *verb,* to counsel

adverse . . . . .opposed, unfavorable
averse . . . . . .unwilling, reluctant

affect . . . . . .*verb,* to influence
effect . . . . . .*noun,* outcome, result
verb, to cause to happen

aid . . . . .help
aide . . . . . . .one who helps

all ready . . . .*adjective,* all prepared
already . . . . .*adverb,* by, before this time

all right . . . .okay
alright . . . . .*disputed spelling!*

Commonly Confused Word Pairs and Homonyms (continued)

allude . . . . . .refer indirectly
elude . . . . . .escape

altar . . . . . . .religious shrine
alter . . . . . . .to change

altogether . .completely
all together .collectively

alumnus . . . .male graduate
alumna . . . .female graduate

anecdote . . .story
antidote . . . .cure for an illness

ascent . . . . . .advancement
assent . . . . . .agree

assure . . . . . .to make confident
ensure . . . . .to make certain
insure . . . . .to buy insurance

attendance . .presence
attendants . .those who attend

B

bail . . . . . . .security for default
bale . . . . . . .corded package of bulky
goods

baring . . . . .exposing
barring . . . . .excluding
bearing . . . . .relating to

beside . . . . . .alongside
besides . . . . .in addition to

biannual . . .twice a year
biennial . . . .every two years

bimonthly . . . . .every two months; *can
mean twice a month
although the preferred
form is . . .*
semimonthly . . .twice a month

birth . . . . .beginning, origin
berth . . . . .a place for sleeping

board . . . . .get into
bored . . . . .weary

born . . . . .brought into being
borne . . . . .carried

bouillon . . . . . . .clear soup
bullion . . . . .uncoined gold or silver

breath . . . . .a vapor
breathe . . . . . . .inhale and exhale

bring . . . . .toward the speaker
take . . . . .away from the speaker

buy . . . . .to purchase
bye . . . . .as in good-bye
by . . . . .not later than, *as in
"Remit by June 1."*

C

can . . . . .capable
may . . . . .asking permission

can not . . . .*wrong spelling*
cannot . . . . .unable

canvas . . . . .heavy cloth
canvass . . . . . . .to poll

Commonly Confused Word Pairs and Homonyms (continued)

casual . . . . .offhand
causal . . . . .relating to cause

censor . . . . .a critic
censure . . . . . . .condemn

cent . . . . .a small coin
sent . . . . .dispatched
scent . . . . .a smell

cereal . . . . .edible grain
serial . . . . .of a series

cession . . . . . . .giving up, surrender
session . . . . . . .regular meeting

choose . . . . . . .select (*present, future tenses*)

chose . . . . .selected

cite . . . . .to quote
site . . . . .a place
sight . . . . .the power of seeing, a view

coalition . . . . . . .an alliance
collision . . . . . . .violent contact
collusion . . . . . .connivance

coarse . . . . .rough
course . . . . . . .direction taken

complaint . . . . .statement of grievance
complainant . . .one who complains
compliant . . . . .docile, yielding

complement . . .*noun,* something that completes
compliment . . . .*noun,* flattery
verb, to praise

comprehensible . . . .understandable
comprehensive . . . . .covering much

confidant . . . . .one to whom a secret is told

confident . . . . .assured

conscience . . . . .sense of right and wrong

conscious . . . . .aware

convince . . . . .used with *that*
persuade . . . . .used with *to*

core . . . . .central part
corps . . . . .number of persons acting together
corpse . . . . .dead body

He has a chronicle knee injury.

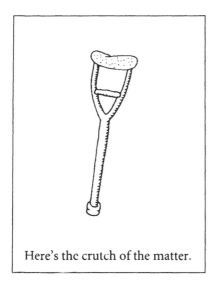

Here's the crutch of the matter.

desert . . . . .abandon
dessert . . . . .final course to a
meal

detract . . . . .take from
distract . . . . .divert

device . . . . .appliance
devise . . . . .contrive

diffuse . . . . .wordy, rambling
defuse . . . . .subdue, soften

disinterested . . . . .impartial
uninterested . . . . .bored

dual . . . . .relating to two
duel . . . . .fight between two

E

elegy . . . . .poem about death
eulogy . . . . .formal praise

elicit . . . . .draw forth
illicit . . . . .illegal

eligible . . . . .qualified
illegible . . . . .unreadable

elusive . . . . .not easily grasped or
defined
illusive . . . . .imaginary

emigrate . . . . . . .leave country
immigrate . . . . . . .enter country

epitaph . . . . .tombstone
inscription
epithet . . . . .descriptive nickname

eraser . . . . .that which
removes
erasure . . . . .act of erasing

corespondent . . . .third party in divorce
action
correspondent . . .letter writer

councilor . . . . . . .council member
counselor . . . . . . .one who gives advice

covert . . . .*adjective,* secret
overt . . . .*adjective,* open

currant . . . . .a berry
current . . . . .recent

D

depreciate . . . . . .lessen in value
deprecate . . . . . .express disapproval

descent . . . . .downward movement
decent . . . . .proper, fitting
dissent . . . . .disagree

Commonly Confused Word Pairs and Homonyms *(continued)*

except . . . . *see* accept
accept

extant . . . . existing at large
extent . . . . scope

F

fair . . . . equitable
fare . . . . cost of a trip

farther . . . . . . refers to physical distance
further . . . . . . refers to degree or extent

feat . . . . an act of skill
feet . . . . units of measure

fewer . . . . individual, countable
     items
less . . . . bulk or quantity

fore . . . . *prefix,* ahead of
four . . . . the number 4

formally . . . . . according to strict rules
formerly . . . . . previously

forth . . . . forward
fourth . . . . . . *as in* Fourth of July

freeze . . . . . . to chill, immobilize
frieze . . . . . . ornamental band, as in
     architecture

G

gait . . . . manner of walking
gate . . . . door

gorilla . . . . . . a kind of ape
guerrilla . . . . . irregular warfare

guessed . . . . . estimated
guest . . . . a visitor

H-I-J

here . . . . in this place
hear . . . . to listen

hoard . . . . . . secret treasure
horde . . . . . . a crowd

hole . . . . opening, cavity
whole . . . . . . all

holy . . . . sinless
wholly . . . . . completely

hoping . . . . . . desiring
hopping . . . . leaping

human . . . . . . a person
humane . . . . . compassionate, kind

idle . . . . inactive
idol . . . . a person or statue
     worshipped

imply . . . . to suggest
infer . . . . to deduce from
     evidence

indigenous . . . native to an area, inborn,
     inherent
indigent . . . . . poor

ingenious . . . . skillful, clever
ingenuous . . . candid, artless

its . . . . possessive form of *it*
it's . . . . contraction of *it is* or *it
     has*

K-L-M-N

know . . . . .be aware

no . . . . .negative

later . . . . .opposite of earlier

latter . . . . . . .opposite of former

lay . . . . .takes an object, *as in*
"Lay the report on my
desk."

lie . . . . .does not take an object,
as in "The report was
lying on my desk."

lead . . . . .a metal

led . . . . .guided

liable . . . . .legally responsible

libel . . . . .written slander

magnet . . . . . . .something that
attracts

magnate . . . . .person of power

main . . . . .primary

mane . . . . . . .long hair on neck of
animal

moot . . . . .debatable

mute . . . . .silent

moral . . . . . . .relating to ethics

morale . . . . . . .mental attitude

O-P

ordinance . . . . .local law

ordnance . . . . .military equipment

passed . . . .*verb,* went by

past . . . .*noun/adjective,* previous

peak . . . . .projecting point

peek . . . . .look

pique . . . . . . .annoy

persecute . . . . .mistreat

prosecute . . . . .sue

personal . . . . . .private

personnel . . . .group of persons
employed

perspective . . . .*noun,* viewpoint

prospective . . .*adjective,* potential,
probable

My sister uses massacre on her eyes.

Commonly Confused Word Pairs and Homonyms (continued)

plain . . . . .straightforward

plane . . . . .flat surface

preposition . . . .part of speech

proposition . . . .plan

principal . . . . . .main, chief,
                   superintendent

principle . . . . . .rule, standard

proceed . . . . . . .continue

precede . . . . . . .go before

prostate . . . . . . .a male gland

prostrate . . . . . .prone

pseudo . . . .*prefix,* fictitious

quasi . . . .*prefix,* in part, partially

Q-R

quiet . . . . .free of noise

quite . . . . .completely

raise . . . . .lift

raze . . . . .demolish

respectfully . . . .with respect

respectively . . . .in the order given

rest . . . . .remain still

wrest . . . . .snatch, twist away from

He can tell you all the perpendiculars of the matter.

right . . . . .correct

rite . . . . .a ceremony

write . . . . .to compose with words

wright . . . . .a mechanic or builder

role . . . . .part one plays

roll . . . . .an official list

S-T-U

soul . . . . .spirit

sole . . . . .only

stationary . . . . .*adjective,* fixed in place

stationery . . . . .*noun,* writing paper

statue . . . . .sculpted figure

statute . . . . . . .law, rule

tale . . . . .a story

tail . . . . .hindmost part of an animal

than . . . . .after a comparison, *as in "Go with John rather than Joe."*

then . . . . .indicating time, next

their . . . . .possessive, as in *"their contract"*

there . . . . .in that place

they're . . . . . . .contraction of *they are*

threw . . . . .hurled

through . . . . . . .in one side and out the other

I have put a preposition before the committee.

Commonly Confused Word Pairs and Homonyms (continued)

too . . . . .also, excess

two . . . . . . .a pair, the number 2

to . . . .*as in "Report to the office."*

V-W-X-Y-Z

vain . . . . . . .futile, conceited

vane . . . . . . .wind-direction indicator

vein . . . . . . .a blood vessel, a distinctive trait

vice . . . . . . .depravity

vise . . . . . . .a gripping tool

weather . . . .atmospheric conditions

whether . . . .*as in "whether I will accept"*

whole . . . . . .*see* hole
hole

wholly . . . . .*see* holy
holy

whose . . . . . .*as in "Whose client?"*

who's . . . . . .contraction of *who is*

your . . . .*as in "your credentials"*

you're . . . . . .contraction of *you are*

7. Sloppy Poofreading . . . er, Proofreading

How embarrassing years ago when a *Good Morning, America* host left little doubt about his feelings for his sponsor when he announced: "We'll be right back after this word from General Fools."

And how embarrassing for the district manager who requested financial support from corporate headquarters to sponsor a stickball tournament in his district. The e-mail that reached headquarters, however, requested funding for a spitball tournament!

Fortunately, the DM's fate was not the same as that of the Russian typesetter during Stalin's reign who misprinted the leader's name as *Salin,* meaning "pigface." Failing to proofread cost that man his life. Let's hope the most it ever costs you is your pride.

Any memo, letter, or report that bears your signature is your, *not* your assistant's, responsibility.

Computer spell checkers do their/they're/there part, but they can't tell/tail/tale you if the word makes cents/sense in the sentence that its/it's in. In the end it's up to you!

Beware the following linguistic gaffes others were not so fortunate to avoid:

From the classifieds:

> "Our experienced mom will care for your child. Fenced yard, meals, and smacks included."

From church bulletins:

> "The rosebud on the altar this morning is to announce the birth of David Alan Belser, the sin of the Reverend and Mrs. Julius Belser."

> "During the pastor's vacation absence, the deacons will arrange for pastoral cuties."

"The first Communion service of the New Year will be held next Sunday. Why not start the New Year tight?"

From a school note written by a parent:

"Please excuse Joey Friday. He had loose vowels."

From the Travel section of a newspaper:

"There are more golf curses in North Carolina than anywhere else in the world."

From a wedding invitation:

"Marie and Jack Capano request the honor of your presents at the marriage of . . ."

From a resumé cover letter:

"I received my graduate degree in unclear physics."

The Spell Checker Poem

I have a spelling checker,
It cam with my PC,
It clearly markes for my revue,
Mistakes I cannot sea.
I've run this poem threw it,
I'm sure your pleased to no.
Its letter perfect in it's weigh—
My spell check tolled me sew.
Anonymous

BUNGLE RULES

Though grammar in writing is no laughing matter, it is worth a chuckle now and then—especially if the chuckle makes the rules of usage easier to remember.

Here's a collection of clever uses and misuses for you to review. Enjoy!

- The adverb always follows the verb.
- Remember to never split an infinitive. It is wrong to ever do so.
- The passive voice should never be used.
- Avoid run-on sentences they are hard to read.
- Don't use no double negatives.
- Use the semicolon properly, always use it where it is appropriate; and never where it isn't.
- "Avoid overuse of 'quotation marks' " in sentences.
- Reserve the apostrophe for it's proper use and omit it when its not needed.
- Do not put statements in the negative form.
- Take care that your subject and verb is in agreement.
- Don't obfuscate your memo with extraneous verbiage.
- No sentence fragments.
  Corollary: complete sentences: important
- Proofread carefully to see if you any words out.
- Avoid commas, that aren't necessary.
- If you reread your work, you will find in rereading that a great deal of repetition can be avoided by rereading and editing. In conclusion, never ever use repetitive redundancies. Remember, stamp out and eliminate redundancy.
- A writer must not shift your point of view.
- Eschew dialect, irregardless.
- And don't start a sentence with a conjunction.
- Don't overuse exclamation points!!!!
- Place pronouns as close as possible, especially in long sentences, such as those of ten or more words, to their antecedents.

- Hyphenate between syllables, and avoid un-necessary hyphens.
- One should never generalize.
- Be more or less specific.
- Foreign words and phrases have a certain *je ne sais quoi*, but are usually not apropos.
- Parenthetical remarks (however relevant) are unnecessary.
- Eschew ampersands & abbreviations, etc.
- Prepositions are not words to end sentences with.
- Write all adverbial forms correct.
- Don't use contractions in formal writing. They aren't necessary.
- Writing carefully, dangling participles must be avoided.
- It is incumbent on us to avoid archaisms.
- If any word is improper at the end of a sentence, a linking verb is.
- Steer clear of incorrect forms of verbs that have sprang into the language.
- Never go off on tangents, which are lines that intersect a curve at only one point and were discovered by Euclid, who lived in the sixth century, which was an era dominated by the Goths, who lived in what we now know as Poland. . . .
- Puns are for children, not groan adults.
- One word sentence? Eliminate.
- Be careful to use the rite homonym.
- Everyone should be careful to use a singular pronoun with singular nouns in their writing.
- Take the bull by the hand and avoid mixed metaphors.
- Avoid trendy locutions that sound flaky and like totally cool, groovy slang.
- If I've told you once, I've told you a thousand times, resist hyperbole. Exaggeration is a million times worse than understatement.
- Also, avoid awkward or affected alliteration. Always.
- Don't string too many prepositional phrases together unless you are walking through the valley of the shadow of death.
- Always pick on the correct idiom.
- Eliminate overuse of quotations. As Emerson said, "I hate quotations. Tell me what you know."

- Profanity sucks.
- Understatement is always best.
- Who needs rhetorical questions?
- Last but not least, avoid clichés like the plague; they are old hat. Seek viable alternatives.

FREQUENTLY ASKED QUESTIONS ABOUT GRAMMAR . . . AND THEIR ANSWERS

QUESTION: WHAT'S THE DIFFERENCE BETWEEN *LIKE* AND *AS*?

The infamous ad slogan "Winston tastes good like a cigarette should" has long been touted as ungrammatical. But why? Here's the long-held rule:

- Use *like* when a phrase follows.
- Use *as* when a verb clause follows.

  Examples: Winston tastes good as a cigarette should.

  "I float like a butterfly, sting like a bee."—Muhammad Ali

QUESTION: WHAT'S THE DIFFERENCE BETWEEN *E.G.* AND *I.E.*?

- e.g. comes from *exempli gratia*, the Latin for "for example."
- i.e. comes from *id est*, the Latin for "that is to say."

Whichever you use, place a comma both before the abbreviation and after the second period.

QUESTION: WHEN DO YOU USE *WHO* AND *WHOM*?

- Who takes the place of *he* or *she*; it's a subject in the sentence.
- Whom takes the place of *him, her*, or *them*; it's an object in the sentence.

Try substituting he/she or him/her when you are deciding. You'll know which is correct by what sounds right.

  Examples: Whom (her/him) are you writing to? (I am writing to *him*.)

  He is a CEO whom (him) we all admire. (We all admire *him*.)

QUESTION: IF YOU HAVE TWO CONSECUTIVE ADJECTIVES, DO YOU ALWAYS HAVE A COMMA BETWEEN THEM?

In "The new computer has a small, attractive footprint" the comma takes the place of *and*. When two consecutive adjectives both describe the noun, use a comma.

Examples: The stock took a quick, unexpected dip.

But when one of the adjectives describes the other, no comma is needed.

Examples: On the cab ride to the office, I stared at the pale blue sky.

QUESTION: DO YOU HAVE ANY OTHER QUICK HINTS FOR WHEN TO USE WHAT PUNCTUATION?

- The **comma**, often used at the writer's discretion, indicates a brief pause or clarifies meaning. Four common uses are

  1. to separate an introductory phrase or clause from the rest of the sentence
  2. to separate independent sentences joined by a conjunction
  3. to distinguish items in a series
  4. to set off added information embedded in a sentence.

- The **semicolon** indicates a long pause; it is most frequently used, as in this sentence, to separate closely related clauses not linked by a conjunction.

- The **colon** indicates a full stop to signify that an explanation or a list follows. Also, in business correspondence, the colon follows the "Dear—" line.

- The **dash**—a short straight line—emphasizes a point by separating it from the rest of the sentence. It is used to indicate an abrupt change or to set off explanatory words or phrases. Used with care in business writing, the dash provides a dramatic pause.

- The **ellipsis** . . . tells us something is missing from a quote. If used sparingly, it also can serve as does the dash . . . to emphasize.

- **Parentheses** de-emphasize information (unlike dashes, which call attention to the point being made).

- Though more a design element than a punctuation mark, the **bullet**
  - emphasizes a point by setting it off from the rest of the text
  - makes information more readable
  - is a substitute for numbering items in a list, especially when a specific sequence is not important.

QUESTION: WHICH IS RIGHT: "I FEEL GOOD" OR "I FEEL WELL"?

- "I feel good" is correct if you're talking about your health. *Good* is an adjective describing *I*.

- "I feel well" is correct if you're talking about the efficiency with which you feel something. *Well* is an adverb describing *feel*.

QUESTION: WHICH IS CORRECT—*A* HISTORICAL OR *AN* HISTORICAL?

While "an historic moment" and "an Hispanic community" sound right, they aren't. For centuries many *h*'s were unaspirated (unsounded), so writers and speakers placed *an* in front of words like *historian*. Today still, the *h* is silent in words like *hour* and *honest*, requiring an *an* before them. However, when the *h* is aspirated (as in *holiday*), place *a*, not *an* in front of it.

The rule applies to how the word is pronounced: Use *a* before words beginning with a consonant sound; use *an* for words beginning with a vowel sound.

QUESTION: HOW DO YOU WRITE THE SALUTATION IN A LETTER WHEN YOU DON'T KNOW THE NAME OF THE PERSON YOU'RE WRITING TO?

Try, try, try to get the name. If you can't discover the precise person who'll read your letter, address the function (customer-relations rep), *not* the department.

"Dear Sir or Madam" ranks today as a cliché, and "To Whom It May Concern" rarely concerns anyone. Omit them.

QUESTION: IS THERE A DIFFERENCE BETWEEN *WHICH* AND *THAT*?

Yes, but not a much-adhered-to difference today. *Which* is considered a non-restrictive modifier, meaning it is used to add nonessential information to a sentence. It inserts such information with the help of commas.

Example: The chair, which was badly soiled, was removed from the lobby.

On the other hand, *that* is used to add essential information to the sentence. No commas needed here.

Example: The chair that was badly soiled was removed from the lobby.
(In this case, the clause "that was badly soiled" is critical to the sentence.)

Here's another situation where *that* is correct.

Example: The mission statement that was approved by the department was forwarded to the CEO.

An even better way to avoid the that/which dilemma is to remove these clauses from your writing altogether.

Examples: The badly soiled chair was removed from the lobby.
The approved mission statement was forwarded to the CEO.

QUESTION: DO YOU USE A POSSESSIVE PRONOUN IN FRONT OF AN "-ING" WORD?

Yes, usually; "-ing" words, formally known as gerunds, take a possessive.

Examples: The boss didn't like *my being* late for the meeting.
(Versus *me*)
The team supported *her/Jane's* prepar*ing* the slides in-house.
(Versus *Jane.*)

QUESTION: WHEN DO YOU HYPHENATE WORDS?

Be guided by (1) the dictionary and (2) the goal of preventing misreading.

Example: The facilities manager ordered a new Widget 1000 forklift that comes complete with five position indicators.
(Five position indicators came with it.)

> versus
>
> The facilities manager ordered a new Widget 1000 forklift that comes complete with five-position indicators.
>
> (These are indicators with five positions on them.)

Generally, when you are treating several words as one unit, you can hyphenate.

Examples: over-the-hill
know-how
stick-to-itiveness
ready-to-wear
faster-than-expected production

When you are using the unit as an adjective, hyphenate only when the words appear *before* the noun they modify.

Example: It was a fast-paced meeting.

> versus
>
> The meeting was fast paced.

Also, when an adverb ending in "ly" modifies an adjective, don't hyphenate them.

Incorrect: We are required to attend all regularly-scheduled meetings.

Correct: We are required to attend all regularly scheduled meetings.

When in doubt, check a current dictionary.

FORMAL GRAMMAR RULES YOU CAN BEND

QUESTION: AREN'T THERE ANY GRAMMAR RULES THAT I CAN BEND?

Indeed! Try these.

- Ending a Sentence with a Preposition (to sound more natural)

Though Winston Churchill said, "Ending a sentence with a preposition is a practice up with which I will not put," don't always heed his tongue-in-cheek advice. Be natural first.

- This is a new technology we are familiar with.
- The survey will indicate where most of our orders are coming from.

- The company encountered competition it wasn't prepared for.
- What are you thinking about?
- Whom did you speak to?

And how's this, from a child to her parent:

- "What did you bring a book I didn't want to be read from out of up for?"

■ **Beginning a Sentence with *And*** (to call attention to your point)

- We're number one in the industry. And we're proud of it.
- "And there was evening, and there was morning—the sixth day."
- "And God said, 'Let there be light,' and there was light."
- . . . managing small plants is easier. And they get better workers because their size enables them to be more selective.

■ **Beginning a Sentence with *But*** (to signal your reader to the difference you are pointing out)

- We thought Grenada was an island paradise. But it wasn't.
- The battle against inflation is constant. But, for once, we seem to be winning.
- John has seventeen parking tickets. But who's counting?

■ **Beginning a Sentence with *Because*** (to vary your sentence beginnings and avoid monotony in reading)

- Because the competition is closing in, we need to consider additional pricing promotions.
- Because time and tide wait for no one, we'd better get moving.
- Because she didn't understand the rules, she lost the game.

■ **Splitting an Infinitive** (to create a special emphasis)

- I cannot bring myself to fully like the candidate.
- I decided to—now and forever—stop smoking.
- The new beer will allow us to greatly increase our profit.

Ever since the starship *Enterprise* set out "to boldly go where no man has gone before," split infinitives have shown up everywhere. Bear in mind, however, to frequently split them is to excessively tax your reader's patience, which a good writer tries to never do.

When you can unsplit by just switching, do so.

Split: I want to carefully examine the code dates.

Unsplit: I want to examine the code dates carefully.

But, *keep* the infinitive split when to do otherwise would create awkwardness.

Example: To really understand calculus's differential equations, you need Ms. Marquez as an instructor.

- **Using a Sentence Fragment** (again, for emphasis, variety, or compactness)

  - Will their company win? Not on your life.
  - Our guarantee is good for one year. Without exception.
  - The problem is that beer doesn't get sold that way. Especially cans with out-of-code dates.
  - What would it take to get you to run for office? Asking, for starters.

Use sparingly. When you do, keep the fragment short so your reader will know you used it deliberately. Fragments can provide a stylistic flair and thus are useful. Sometimes, anyway.

- **Using a Contraction** (to sound conversational)

  - I've completed a new study for you to review.
  - The plant hasn't experienced an accident in two hundred days.
  - Why wasn't Sharon promoted?
  - Who's there? It's Tom, let's hope.

12
Spelling

WHAT IF YOU'RE A LOUSY SPELLER?

Once you've checked your content and your grammar, check carefully the surface features (spelling, punctuation, capitalization, spacing).

And if you're a lousy speller, you're in good company. Neither Thomas Edison nor Abe Lincoln could spell well; and, by his own admission, neither can author John Irving. It's little wonder. There are so many rules. What's worse—there are exceptions to every one of them.

George Bernard Shaw quipped about the foolishness of spelling rules. Using them, he said, *fish* could be spelled "ghoti." Simply take the *f* as it sounds in *enough*; the *i* as it sounds in *women*; and the *sh* as it sounds in *fiction*. Actually, the *sh* sound can be written in more than a dozen other ways as well:

- shot
- issue
- sugar
- ocean
- fuchsia
- coercion
- conscience
- cremation
- schnapps
- pshaw
- chagrin
- procession
- nauseous

Where did such a mess of possibilities come from? We can find out by taking the word *debt* as an example. Derived from the Old French *dette* or *dete*, the *b* was added to both the English and French spellings in the late Middle Ages by scholars who wished the word to reflect its origin from the Latin word *debitum*. The French form has since removed the *b* while the English spelling has maintained it, giving millions of schoolchildren yet another silent letter that must be memorized. Similar tales of alterations in spelling explain these words: *plumb, subtle, indict, receipt, island, isle,* and *aisle.*

But we can look at the spelling dilemma from a positive perspective. Ninety percent of what is written consists of only a thousand basic words. Doesn't that make you feel better? Kidding aside, what, if anything, can you do to improve poor spelling? Perhaps the best cure for bad spelling is lots of good reading. Keep your mind alert to the look of the words.

Second, use a dictionary. And keep track of the number of times you have to look up the same word (just put a number beside the entry). Now don't respond with that worn-out argument, "How can I look it up if I don't know how to spell it?" Instead, try this: Look up a synonym for the word you can't spell. More than likely, you'll find the word you want to spell under the definition of the synonym.

Third, take advantage of word-processing programs that have a spell-check function. Even e-mail programs offer this function, so be sure to activate it. Faithfully use the spell checker before sending out your memos, reports, and letters. But don't trust it to find all your spelling errors. It isn't smart enough to know you typed "ruin" when you meant "run," "if" when you meant "is," or "beast" when you meant "best." Only you can find these errors . . . preferably before your readers do.

Fourth, a few rules may prove useful. I recommend two books in particular that contain clear explanations and concrete examples: Jan Venolia's *Write Right!* and *Rewrite Right!* (both published by Ten Speed Press/Periwinkle Press).

Remember, while English spelling is not invariable, there is agreement about most words. Granted, a small number of words may be spelled in more than one way. Usually, one of these ways comes to be preferred, and the other is discarded. Occasionally, new, simplified versions are introduced (by a brave few). For instance, a simplified version that has taken hold in our lifetime is *thruway.* It is, as William Strunk states in his classic work, *The Elements of Style,* "a high-speed word for readers who are going seventy. *Throughway* would be too long to fit on a road sign, too slow to serve the speeding eye."

But misspelled words in your business or school writing convey your message in a flawed way. Plus they tell your reader you were too tired or lazy to check. Misspellings are usually met with disfavor. They distract (and sometimes disgust) your reader. Don't risk your reader's wrath. And don't attempt to write *pleez* for *please*, or *nite* for *night* unless you are planning on simplifying your complete spelling system. If you are, be prepared for the consequences.

Easily Misspelled Words

A
* a_lot
  absence
  abundant
  academic
  academically
  acceptable
* accidentally
* accommodate
  accomplish
  accurate
  accustom
* achievement
  acknowledgment
* acquaintance
* acquire
  across
  actual
  actually
  adequately
* admissible
  admission
  admittance
  adolescent

advertise
advertisement
aggravate
aggression
aggressive
* Albuquerque
alleviate
* all right
* amateur
among
analysis
* analyze
annual
* anoint
answer
apologize
apology
* apparent
appearance
* appropriate
approximate
arctic
argument
arithmetic

arouse
article
ascent
* assistance
athlete
athletic
attendance
attendant
attitude
audience
authority
* awkward

B
* bachelor
balance
balloon
* bankruptcy
beautiful
beginner
beginning
behavior
believe
* beneficial

* Most frequently misspelled words.

Easily Misspelled Words (continued)

* benefited
  Britain
* bureaucracy
  business

C

* calendar
* canceled
  candidate
  capitalism
  career
* Caribbean
  category
* changeable
  characteristic
  chief
  choice
* Cincinnati
* coincidence
  coming
  commercial
  commission
* commitment
  committee
  comparative
  compatible
  compelled
  competition
  competitive
  competitor

  complete
  concede
  conceivable
  conceive
  concentrate
  conferred
* connoisseur
  connotation
* conscientious
* conscious
* consensus
  consequently
  considerably
  consistent
  continuously
* controlled
  controlling
  controversial
  convenient
  coolly
  correlate
  courtesy
* criticism
  criticize
  curiosity

D

* deceive
  decision
* deductible

* defendant
  deferred
  definitely
  dependent
* descendant
  description
* Des Moines
  dictionary
  difference
* dilemma
* disappoint
  disastrous
  discipline
  discriminate
* dissimilar
  doesn't
  dominant
* dossier
  during

E

* easily
  ecstasy
* efficient
* eighth
* eligible
  eliminate
* embarrass
* emphasize
  encouraging

* Most frequently misspelled words.

Easily Misspelled Words (continued)

enough
enthusiasm
entirely
* entrepreneur
* enumerate
* environment
equipped
equivalent
especially
* exaggerate
excellent
experience
experiment
explanation
* extraordinary
extremely

F
* facsimile
fallacy
* familiar
* fascinate
February
finally
* foreign
forty
frantically
friend
* fulfill
fundamentally

G
gaiety
* gauge
generally
genius
government
governor
* grammar
grammatically
grandeur
grievous
* guarantee
guidance

H
* harass
height
* hemorrhage
* hindrance
humorous
* hypocrite

I
ideally
ignorant
* illogical
immediate
* impasse
* inadvertent
* incidentally

* indispensable
inevitable
influence
influential
ingenious
initiate
* innuendo
inoculate
intelligent
interest
interpretation
interrupt
* irrelevant
irresistible
* itinerary

J
January
* judgment

K
Kleenex
* knowledge
knowledgeable

L
laboratory
laid
* leisurely
length

* Most frequently misspelled words.

Easily Misspelled Words (continued)

* license
* lien
* likable
* liveliest
  loneliness
* loose
* lose

M

  magazine
  magnificence
  magnificent
* maintenance
* maneuver
  manufacture
  marriage
  mathematics
* mediocre
  Mediterranean
  memento
  merely
* mileage
  millennium
  mischief
  mischievous
  misspell
  misspelling
* mortgage
  mysterious

N

  naturally
* necessary
  necessity
* nickel
* ninety
* ninth
* noticeable
* nuclear

O

* obsolescent
* occasionally
  occur
  occurred
* occurrence
  occurring
* omission
  omitted
  operator
  opinion
  opportunity
  oppose
  optimistic
  original

P

* pamphlet
* parallel

  paralyze
  particular
* pastime
  peculiar
  perceive
  performance
  permanent
* permissible
* perseverance
* persistent
* persuade
  philosophy
  physical
* Pittsburgh
* plausible
  pleasant
  possess
  possibility
  practically
* preceding
  prefer
  preference
  preferred
  prejudice
  preparation
  presence
* privilege
  professor
* programmed

* Most frequently misspelled words.

Easily Misspelled Words (continued)

prominent
* pronunciation
propaganda
* psychiatric
pursue

Q
* quantity
* questionnaire
* queue
quiet

R
readily
realistically
realize
really
* receipt
receive
* recognize
refer
* reference
referring
relieve
reminisce
* Renaissance
repetition
* rescind
* resistance
* rhythm

S
sacrifice
* salable
salary
* satellite
scarcity
secretary
* seize
* separate
several
severely
* siege
* simultaneous
sincerely
* sizable
specifically
sponsor
straight
strength
* subpoena
substantial
subtle
* subtly
succeed
success
sufficient
summary
suppose
suppress

* surprise
* susceptible

T
* technique
* temperament
theory
* thorough
* threshold
tomorrow
* tragedy
* transferred
traveled
traveler
tries
truly
Tuesday

U
* unanimous
undoubtedly
unnecessary
unusually
* unwieldy

V
* vacillate
* vacuum
valuable
vengeance

* Most frequently misspelled words.

Easily Misspelled Words (continued)

W	X	Z
wa<u>rr</u>ant	<u>X</u>erox	zer<u>o</u>
* We<u>d</u>nesday		
* who<u>ll</u>y	**Y**	
wri<u>t</u>ing	* y<u>ie</u>ld	

*Most frequently misspelled words.

FORMING PLURALS FROM OUR STRANGE LANGUAGE

We'll begin with a box and the plural is boxes,
But the plural of ox is oxen, not oxes.
Then one fowl is a goose but two are called geese,
Yet the plural of moose should never be meese.

You find a lone mouse or a whole set of mice,
Yet the plural of house is houses not hice.
If the plural of man is always called men,
Why shouldn't the plural of pan be called pen?

If I speak of a foot and you show me your feet,
And I give you a boot, would a pair be called beet?
If one is a tooth and a whole set are teeth,
Why shouldn't the plural of booth be called beeth?

Then, one may be that, and three would be those,
Yet hat in the plural wouldn't be hose.
We speak of a brother and also say brethren,
But though we say Mother, we never say Methren.

Then, the masculine pronouns are he, his, and him,
But imagine the feminine she, shis, and shim.
So English, I fancy you all will agree,
Is the funniest language you ever did see.

                                         Anonymous

Anonymous said it all. Logic indeed is of limited use in trying to master the rules for forming plurals. While most words take an *s* or *es,* there are enough exceptions to keep us guessing, groaning, or grabbing for the dictionary.

Though not intended to include all the exceptions, the following general guidelines should help explain the cases where a simple *s* won't work.

Forming Plurals

	Singular	Plural	Rule
General rule			
	attorney	attorneys	Add *s* to most nouns.
	memo	memos	
	report	reports	
	zero	zeros	
Nouns ending in . . .			
s	boss	bosses	Add *es.*
x	box	boxes	
z	waltz	waltzes	
ch	bench	benches	
sh	bush	bushes	
***Y* preceded by a consonant**			
	company	companies	Change *y* to *i* and add *es.*
	country	countries	
	family	families	
	story	stories	
What's this rule?			
f	belief	beliefs	For some, add *s.*
	half	halves	For some, change *f* to *v*
	knife	knives	and add *es.*
	loaf	loaves	
	shelf	shelves	
	scarf	scarves, scarfs	Some have two forms.
	wharf	wharves, wharfs	

Forming Plurals (continued)

Singular	Plural	Rule
O preceded by a vowel		
cameo	cameos	Add *s.*
portfolio	portfolios	
ratio	ratios	
studio	studios	
O preceded by a consonant		
echo	echoes	For some, add *es.*
hero	heroes	
tomato	tomatoes	
veto	vetoes	
alto	altos	Add *s.* (Musical terms
banjo	banjos	and other exceptions fall
piano	pianos	under this rule.)
cargo	cargoes, cargos	Some have two forms.
memento	mementos, mementoes	
mosquito	mosquitoes, mosquitos	
Plural nouns		
	pliers	These are always plural.
	remains	
	scissors	
	thanks	
Singular nouns		
linguistics		These are always
mathematics		singular.
news		
physics		
Singular/Plural		
deer	deer	These take the same
information	information	form for both.
moose	moose	
Japanese	Japanese	

Forming Plurals (continued)

Singular	Plural	Rule
Singular/Plural		
child	children	These form in irregular ways.
foot	feet	
goose	geese	
mouse	mice	
ox	oxen	
tooth	teeth	
woman	women	
Compound nouns		
attorney-at-law	attorneys-at-law	Change the principal word (make the noun plural).
by-product	by-products	
notary public	notaries public	
Acronyms and numbers		
VIP	VIPs	Add *s* (but no apostrophe unless you're forming a possessive).
	1990s	
COD	CODs	Add *s* or change the construction to make reading easier.
IOU	IOUs	
two	twos	
2×4	2×4s	
Words derived from foreign words		
addendum	addenda	Form as in original language.
alumna	alumnae (fem.)	
alumnus	alumni	
analysis	analyses	
crisis	crises	
criterion	criteria	
datum	data	
hypothesis	hypotheses	

Forming Plurals (continued)

Singular	Plural	Rule
Words derived from foreign words		
medium	media	Form as in original language.
nucleus	nuclei	
phenomenon	phenomena	

A Word About Trademarks

If you work for a company with a product line, know what products are registered trademarks. And then protect those trademarks—and the trademarks of others—by identifying them appropriately in all your correspondence. It's your way of showing respect for others' products and pride in your own.

For example:

Kleenex® products   Coke®

Gore-tex® fabrics   Windex® cleaner

Velcro® brands   Milky Way® brand bar

The general rule is to use the TM or ® symbol the first time you write the product name on a page. But check your company's product list and style guide to comply to their accepted practice.

Part 6 Writing Quickly and Well

The blankness of the writing surface may cause the mind to shy. It may be impossible to release the faculties. Write, write anything: It is in all probability worthless anyhow . . . But it is absolutely essential to the writing of anything worthwhile that the mind be fluid and release itself to the task.

William Carlos Williams

13

Deadline Writing: A Process for Getting It Started, Keeping It Going, Getting It Right

By now you have a strong sense of what good writing is and how to accomplish it. Yet I can hear you grumble, "But at work I need to write not only well, but also quickly. Can I accomplish both?" The answer is yes.

The writing-for-deadlines method takes whatever time you can allot to your writing project and forces you to focus on one phase of it at a time—guaranteeing you won't shortchange (or omit) any phase of the process. This method helps control both your time and the quality of the work you produce during it. It's especially useful when you don't have lots of time to get the writing done and when routine correspondence has piled up. Some think of it as a let's-get-this-over-with approach to writing. Whatever you call it, you'll find it powerful. It allows the writing to evolve, to grow, even within a tight time frame. This technique works whether you compose directly on the computer or prefer to draft first by hand.

Here's the writing-for-deadlines method—and a Quick-Draft Form to help you try the technique on your next piece of work-related writing.

PHASE ONE: HELTER-SKELTER WRITING— THE ZERO DRAFT

1. Write down everything you *think* you may want to say about your topic—fast: your hunches, insights, all the data you can think of. Speed has value. Resist separating the writing—or typing—from the thinking at this stage.

2. Use no energies organizing, editing.

3. If you can't find the right word, leave a blank.

4. If you can't say it the right way, for now say it the "wrong" way.

5. If you see you're going off the track, skip lines and start again.

6. If you find yourself repeating, skip lines and start again.

7. If a new idea pops in while you're working on another one . . .

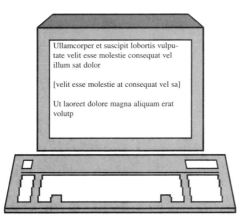

Ullamcorper et suscipit lobortis vulpu-
tate velit esse molestie consequat vel
illum sat dolor

[velit esse molestie at consequat vel sa]

Ut laoreet dolore magna aliquam erat
volutp

. . . write it on the screen or in the margin and continue with your original thought.

If it won't go away, stop and develop it. Then go back to your original idea.

You can also substitute any of the fourteen "Getting Started" strategies (see pages 18 to 21) as your helter-skelter phase.

Helter-Skelter Zero Draft Version

Dear Al,

Bob Tipton began his business career with Best Corp. I've interviewed & referenced Bob and feel that despite his recent job change, he's worth considering for the VP marketing.

[seasned sales manager with marketing know-how]

I sense in talking with him that his present position with Exton is comparatively limited & so not as challinging an assinment as he would like to have.

He's in good health, married and has 2 children. He's articulate, pleasant, alert, self-assured, outspoken. Ambitious to get ahead by taking on more responsibility. He's 38 yrs. old & says his compensation is flexible.

Bob joined Brunswick Corp. as a sales rep three years later. Became disgusted with co's growth planning process and landed a corporate planning position with Del Rosse, a small co. in the Southwest. It failed soon after he decided to accept a position with Exton.

[completely familiar with the industry]

References check out. a hard worker. Has real integirty. Excellent appearance also.

Resume detailing his experience enclosed.

PHASE TWO: HOCUS-POCUS ORGANIZING

1. Find your focus—the central point you want to make—by asking yourself, "What is the single thing I am trying to say here?"

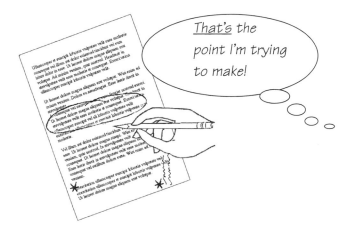

2. If you haven't said it, figure it out now.

3. Find the good points (not necessarily the good writing—we'll do that later). These are the ideas and data that belong in the final version.

4. Arrange the parts. Have the courage to omit material you thought was important but really isn't.

5. Work out your train of thought logically, and where it seems some elements in that pattern are missing, insert them.

6. Generate subheadings if appropriate, so your reader can work through your train of thought or retrieve information quickly.

7. Position your major message so it is accessible up front for your busy reader and generate an engaging subject line.

Hocus-Pocus-Organizing Version

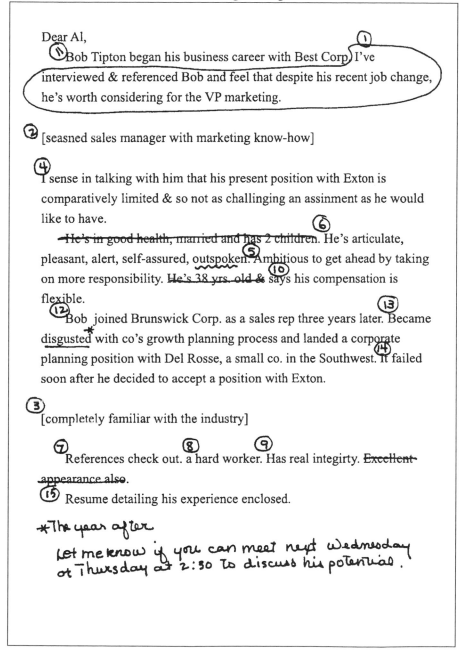

Dear Al,

① Bob Tipton began his business career with Best Corp. I've interviewed & referenced Bob and feel that despite his recent job change, he's worth considering for the VP marketing.

② [seasned sales manager with marketing know-how]

④ I sense in talking with him that his present position with Exton is comparatively limited & so not as challinging an assinment as he would like to have.

~~He's in good health, married and has 2 children.~~ ⑥ He's articulate, pleasant, alert, self-assured, outspoken. ⑤ Ambitious to get ahead by taking on more responsibility. ⑩ ~~He's 38 yrs. old &~~ says his compensation is flexible.

⑫ Bob joined Brunswick Corp. as a sales rep three years later. ⑬ Became disgusted* with co's growth planning process and landed a corporate planning position with Del Rosse, a small co. in the Southwest. ⑭ It failed soon after he decided to accept a position with Exton.

③ [completely familiar with the industry]

⑦ References check out. ⑧ a hard worker. ⑨ Has real integirty. ~~Excellent appearance also.~~

⑮ Resume detailing his experience enclosed.

*The year after
  Let me know if you can meet next Wednesday
  or Thursday at 2:30 to discuss his potential.

PHASE THREE: RUTHLESS EDITING

1. Take your hard copy. Yes, even if you've drafted on the computer, print it out. You'll find editing from hard copy versus your computer screen worthwhile.

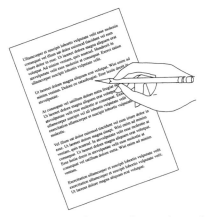

2. And pay attention to *how* you're saying *what* you have to say.

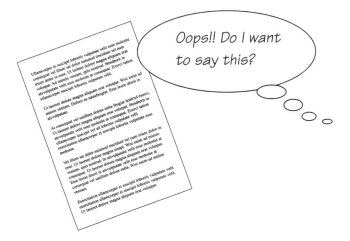

3. Write clearer, fresher sentences for your reader. Now that you've clarified thoughts for yourself, this will be easier to do.

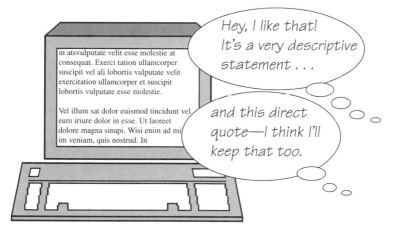

4. Edit for confidence and clarity.

■ Take responsibility and be specific.

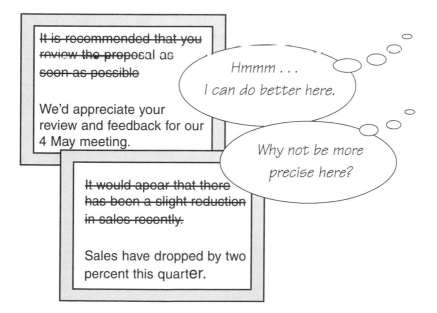

■ Drop vague and vogue language.

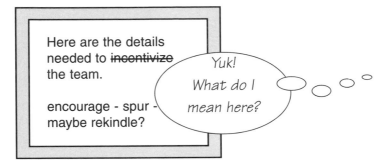

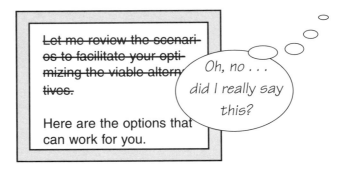

- Delete dull or unnecessary intensifiers.

- Dismiss do-little verbs.

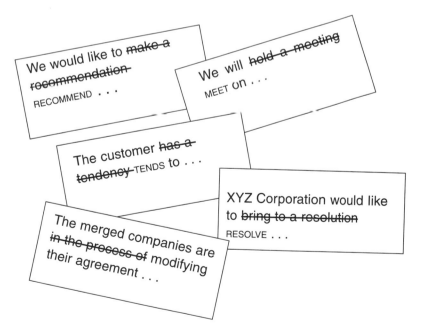

5. Edit for conciseness.

- Get rid of clutter and tighten your writing.

~~There are three options for us to definitely consider.~~
WE HAVE THREE OPTIONS.

~~It is important to note that~~ snack size sales are skyrocketing.

~~It has come to my attention that~~ we have lost momentum in Arizona.

Hmm . . . these sentence starters can go!

~~I thought you would like to know that~~ we have six out of seven people in our region over 100 percent of their service target.

~~Ken, I'm pleased to let you know that~~ I have the promotional items you requested.

~~I would truly like to~~ thank ~~each of~~ you for doing your part to make this happen.

... more clutter

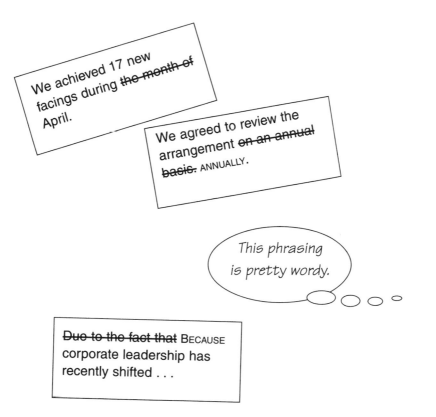

6. Edit for tone/consideration.

- Ban businessese, legalese, parentese, pretentious, condescending, negative, and outdated—or faddish—language.

~~We acknowledge receipt of~~
WE RECEIVED . . .

Paul,
~~What have you done to control the wild overspending rampant in your department?~~
LET'S MEET FRIDAY TO WORK OUT A PLAN THAT WILL BRING EXPENSES IN LINE WITH THE DEPARTMENT'S BUDGET BEFORE YEAR END.

Hmm . . . how negative-sounding.

. . . ~~pursuant to~~ FOLLOWING your instructions

~~You must~~ PLEASE sign these forms by 15 August.

~~You have failed to send in your payment.~~
ONCE YOUR CHECK IS RECEIVED, YOUR ACCOUNT WILL BE UP TO DATE.

~~As per John's memo,~~ Several events have ~~impacted~~ INFLUENCED consumer buying habits this quarter.

. . . provide ~~new learning to~~ our customers ~~relative to~~ WITH significant category facts, trends, and opportunities.

~~Your immediate attention to this matter is appreciated.~~
YOUR QUICK ATTENTION WILL ENSURE . . .

Is this _me_?
It sounds stuffy and inflated.

We are appreciative of the plethora of opportunities you have given us to interface with you within the parameters of our contractual agreement.
WE APPRECIATE YOUR WILLINGNESS TO WORK WITH US UNDER THE GUIDELINES OF OUR AGREEMENT.

~~I wish to express my~~ Thanks ~~to you~~, John, for responding to our customer so promptly.

■ Inject people, pronouns, contractions to personalize.

7. Edit for correctness.

■ Check pronoun use.

- Check subject-verb agreement.

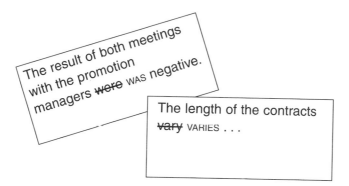

- Check word usage, expecially words that are commonly confused or misspelled . . .

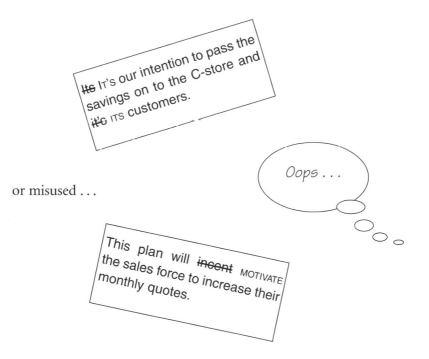

or misused . . .

or used because they sound important.

Let me recapitulate the methodology we will utilize.
IN SUMMARY, THESE ARE THE STEPS WE'LL TAKE.

The candidate is cognizant of the fact KNOWS that you will require relocation . . .

- Check punctuation.

,
As you can see from our reports we are working hard to keep Wanda Job's spirits up and the momentum going.

,
In addition you'll add fresh profits to your confectionery category sales.

Ruthlessly Edited Version

Willa David
Worldwide Search, Inc.
220 West 98th Street
New York, NY 10025

March 3, _____

Alan Beatty, President
XYZ Corporation
1175 Fifth Avenue
New York, NY 10022

Subject: Top Marketing Candidate Identified

Dear Al:

After interviewing Bob Tipton and checking his references, I recommend considering him for the VP Marketing—despite his recent job change. He's a seasoned sales manager with marketing know-how, and he's completely familiar with our industry.

I sense in talking with him that his present position with Exton is comparatively limited and so not as challenging an assignment as he would like to have. Clearly, he's ambitious to get ahead and willing to take on more responsibility. He's articulate, pleasant, alert, self-assured, open. His references agree: he's a hard worker with integrity. Furthermore, he says his compensation is flexible.

Bob began his career with Best Corporation. Three years later he joined Brunswick Corporation as a sales rep. When he became disillusioned with the company's growth-planning process, he landed a corporate-planning position with Del Rosse, a small company in the Southwest. It failed the year after he accepted a position with Exton.

I've enclosed a résumé detailing his work experience and personal background.

Will Wednesday or Thursday at 2:30 be best for us to meet and discuss his potential?

Regards,

Willa

enclosure

Here's a form to help get your first, let's-get-it-over-with draft done. It's intended to invite you to draft quickly and rearrange easily. It will take only a couple of minutes to complete and will provide a useful outline to take with you to the keyboard.

THE QUICK-DRAFT FORM

Subject Line: _____

Bottom-Line Message: _____

Action/Next Steps: _____

Anticipated Reader Reaction: _____

Content in
Key Words

Sequence
of Content
Following
Bottom Line

© *Copyright 1994 Wilma Davidson, Ed. D.*

Part 7 Talking to Other Writers—and to Your Micro Recorder

Writing, when properly managed, is but a different name for conversation.

Laurence Sterne

14
An E-Mail Quick Guide

Every day, employees in large and small companies around the globe face the daunting task of keeping up with the correspondence multiplying in their electronic mailboxes by the nanosecond. Faster than a letter, less costly than a phone call, e-mail is the medium of the millennium. And being able to write e-mail has become an essential work skill. Surely its benefits outweigh its drawbacks: after all, e-mail can eliminate exasperating phone tag; it can, with a keystroke, remove distance and time barriers; conveniently quick, it can reduce isolation, transmit routine administrative details for wide distribution almost effortlessly; and, if not misused, it can increase productivity. So what's not to like about it?

Well, with high stakes and little time, many employees still panic, procrastinate, and perpetuate bad writing habits whenever they create or respond to e-mail. Because the primary benefit of e-mail is its convenience and speed of delivery, it often resembles unedited speech more than polished writing. That is, it tends to have the informal, casual style of chat. This is good—to a degree. But when the speed of response constantly gets preference over the correctness or appropriateness of response, e-mail can help destroy a career. Yes, while generating e-mail can fray nerves, receiving e-mail can antagonize receivers and, ultimately, may lose sales. As a result of these high stakes, a few dos and don'ts are worth considering—whether you are a network newbie or a veteran in cyberspace.

Dos
- **Write an informative and engaging subject line** so your message will be opened first. Instead of "Some Thoughts," try "How to Get and Keep our Edge." Instead of "Meeting Schedule," try "Meeting Rescheduled due to Stork's Early Visit." Subject lines that can stand alone are often the most effective.

- **Bottom-line your message.** That is, position your key point up front on the screen. This keeps the reader reading, and the message clear. Two examples:

  "New Promotion: Get Out and Sell-ebrate"
  "Ready for Countdown for Widget 2100 Launch?"

  Telegraph your key point at the start.

- **Be brief.** Respect other people's time. E-mail messages look and feel twice as long on screen as they do in hard copy. Use short words, phrases, and abbreviations while avoiding being too disjointed or casual. Too abbreviated would be,

  "Pls email yr respnse to me and incl amt needed."

- **Make it easy for your readers to reply.** Word your messages so a yes/no or short answer is possible. Instead of "Let me know what you think," ask "Do you agree?" Instead of "Let's get together to discuss," write, "Is Monday or Wednesday at 2 P.M. better for you?"

- **Make it easy to read.** Use a combination of upper and lower case, white space, and a legible font (Times New Roman, Courier, Arial, Hobo, for example).

It looks like some form of Hieroglyphics. I think it's ancient e-mail.

Make it easy to read.

- **Personalize** by using contractions, pronouns, and a conversational tone.

- **Use symbols** occasionally to emphasize. That *is* a good idea. Use under-scores to indicate underlining._Business Writing: What Works, What Won't_is my favorite book.

- **End well**—with an appropriate next step, a deadline if appropriate, and a positive good will (but not clichéd) comment.

  > "Please respond to the attached questionnaire by
  > Friday, May 10. We welcome your contributions."

- **Proofread** to make sure the speed of e-mail hasn't made you sloppy.

- **Wait a moment before pressing "send."** Be sure your topic, your tone, and your typing won't embarrass you.

- **Make yourself look good online.** Write as if your mother were standing over your shoulder. Remember, your e-mail can easily be forwarded by your recipient to anyone else in the company (or the world).

Write as if your mother were
standing over your shoulder.

Don'ts

- **Don't hide behind your screen.** That is, don't use e-mail to send a message better delivered by another medium. Though quick and convenient, e-mail isn't always appropriate—especially for documents containing performance reviews or disciplinary action. Opt for a phone call or a face-to-face meeting if your message

  - needs to be private or secure;

  - bears unpleasant news;

  - requires immediate response; or

  - could be misunderstood.

Don't hide behind your screen.

- **Don't send an e-mail you wouldn't want anyone else to read.** E-mail can fly around the world with the click of a finger.

- **Don't leave your subject line blank.** A subject line is prime real estate in a business document. Use it as a headline to telegraph your message to your readers. For example, instead of just saying "Quarterly Results," inform your reader with the more-telling "First Quarter Sales Hit All-time High" or "First Quarter Sales Up 4%."

To: ceo@competitors.com

From: vpnumber2@bigbiz.com

Subject: Secret plans for R&D Dept.

Here are the secret designs for our new product. Please deposit my payoff into my Swiss bank account. Delete this message after reading it. If I am caught, it could spell big trouble for me.

I. Spye
Second Assistant VP
Big Buzines Industries

Don't send an e-mail you wouldn't
want anyone else to read.

- **Don't "flame" at your reader.** That is, don't use all capital letters. Besides slowing your reader down, they will heat your reader up because all caps resemble screaming in print.

- **Don't forward messages without a comment.** Put the forwarded material into context—clarify why it's important. The same goes for attachments: Don't say simply, "Please see attached." Instead, tell the reader what the attachment is, and why you're sending it.

  "The attached guidelines explain the incentive contest rules."

  or

  "The attached announcement will introduce you
  to a welcome addition to our management team."

- **Don't overrun your e-mails with smiley faces or other emoticons.** While they may be fun for family and friends, they are less appealing to business associates.

- **Don't let emotions and offensive or sexist language detract from your message.** Sarcasm and swearing not only heat up the screen, they burn your reputation. Be aware that e-mails are easily misconstrued: Something positive might seem sarcastic, or vice versa. Re-read your message for possible alternate meanings.

- **Don't press "send" without checking for mistakes.** While you may be forgiving of others' goofs, they may not react as kindly to yours.

Wait a moment before pressing "send."

15
Collaborating

GIVING FEEDBACK TO OTHERS

No passion in the world is equal to the passion to alter someone else's draft.

H. G. Wells

Writing improves through

1. a writer's own motivation to do better
2. lots and lots of practice
3. good models
4. good feedback.

Giving feedback is a verbal and nonverbal process through which you let others know what you think and feel about something—in this case, about what they've written. Providing such feedback is a critical and time-consuming part of a manager's job. Here's some well-tested advice on giving effective feedback that will help, not hinder, the writer and the writing. It will prove useful whether you're commenting to a subordinate or a coworker.

When you sit down in a feedback session,

Do . . .

- Assume the role of advocate, not adversary.
    - Sit near the writer (but not opposite).
    - Maintain eye contact.
    - Let the writer hold the writing unless it's offered to you.
- Have a clear idea of the major point(s) you want the writer to understand.
    - Research affirms that trying to improve all that may be troublesome in a writing sample (at the same time) may do more harm than good.

Commenting on *everything* wrong at once will fragment the writer's improvement efforts.

Instead, focus on the major problem(s) in the letter, memo, or report. Is it organized logically? Is there enough support for the argument being made? Has the writer stated the purpose for writing up front for the busy business reader?

- Give examples to explain what you mean.

Instead of Saying . . .	*Try . . .*
Disorganized!	Where have you stated your purpose for writing?
	or
	What is your most important point? Why have you placed it there?
	or
	Let's work out an outline together of the order in which this information might be conveyed. Where might you begin? Why?
Awkward!	I'm confused. Are you saying that . . . or . . . ? Do you mean . . . ?
Repetitious!	In wanting to be sure I understood, you told me this point three times in this paragraph. Which one states it best? Which might you remove?

- Mere evaluative comments such as the ones in the left-hand column (whether written or spoken) demean the writer as well as the writing. Furthermore, they don't provide concrete ideas for improving.

  By asking questions rather than flatly asserting, you allow the writer to think through the writing with your guidance rather than your judgments.

- Make your comments easy to understand by using the writer's language and terms.

  - There's nothing to be gained, and much to be lost, by talking over someone's head or using terminology foreign to the person seeking feedback. Explain what you mean plainly and tactfully.

- Pace your feedback to the writer's psychological state of mind.
  - For the writing to improve, you must consider the context in which it is being written. Also, what is that person's present state of mind? Attitude toward writing? Attitude toward what is being written?
- Have a conference in a place where noise and other distractions can be eliminated and at a time when you aren't hurried.
- Set a good example.
  - Care about and create crisp, concise writing yourself.
- Be patient!

Don't . . .

- Talk more than the writer.
  - Letting the writer talk will help clarify that person's thinking.
- Do it for the writer—even if it would be faster.
  - Struggling writers need to stay in the battle if they are to win the war.
- Correct grammatical and structural errors too early in the draft.
  - If you consider where the writer is in the draft, you can limit your comments to the appropriate stage.

    For example, if the writer is still struggling over what points to include or remove, it doesn't make sense for you to correct the draft for spelling and punctuation flaws. After all, some of those words and sentences may not end up in the final report. Curtail the urge to correct those surface features until the content and clarity of the writing have been achieved.

Spoken feedback is preferable to written feedback. It is easier to gauge how you are coming across and to clarify when this is necessary. Face-to-face communication that uses questioning and discussion can help develop and organize ideas. Thus it can be a rich source of guidance.

When an in-person conference is impossible because of travel and meeting schedules, suggest the writer attach the draft to an e-mail to you and write your comments as questions rather than harsh judgments.

A Microsoft Word® document is easy to respond to without hacking it up or merely correcting it. In your copy of the document, just open up TOOLS from the Toolbar and click on TRACK CHANGES, HIGHLIGHT CHANGES, and COMMENTS. Then, as you go through the document, you can create comments that ask the writer to clarify, that raise a question, or that suggest a change.

The writer can review your amended document file with your highlighted comments and be responsible for accepting/rejecting your suggestions. This function in Word even permits several reviewers, and makes it easy for the author to integrate/evaluate everyone's comments.

Before sending their writing out, wise writers recognize the importance of "trying it out" on a real audience—like having a dress rehearsal. When someone asks you to see that rehearsal, remember: The idea is to "break a leg," not a psyche!

A WORD TO THE WISE MANAGER: HOW TO ENCOURAGE EMPLOYEES TO BE RESPONSIBLE FOR THEIR WRITING

Many managers complain that they spend several hours each week rewriting their employees' correspondence because it doesn't say it the way the managers would say it. And countless employees also complain, "How *can* I write for my boss's signature?" No small dilemma. My suggestion to managers: Let your employees write for your endorsement, *not* for your signature.

Why? Because having employees write for your signature disempowers them.

First the manager says, "Prepare a letter for my signature." Then the manager gets the draft, states, "Hm . . . well . . . this isn't what I wanted," and proceeds to rewrite and/or red-pen it to death. The employee sees the totally revised and corrected correspondence and naturally feels demeaned. The scene is repeated often, and the employee, who at first approached the writing task with energy (and some trepidation, perhaps), now barely tries. The employee knows the manager will undoubtedly rewrite whatever is turned in and therefore passes anything along.

Is there a way to break the pattern? Is there a way for the manager to play the advocate and not the adversary in the writing task? And, what is important, is there a way for the writing to improve? Yes. That's what writing-for-endorsement does.

Rather than have employees draft letters that go out under a manager's signature, have employees sign their *own* name to correspondence that has added a manager's endorsement line at the bottom. This endorsement line should signify that the ideas and content are approved by the manager. The endorsement signature, however, need not imply that the manager approves the style or is responsible for any errors.

Style and correctness are the responsibility of the writer. When the manager rewrites, the manager wrests away that responsibility. Managers who constantly rewrite disempower those who work for them. While the writing gets temporarily bandaged, the problem of poor writing doesn't go away.

Significant, long-term benefits accompany adopting a write-for-my-endorsement versus a write-for-my-signature approach:

1. It places the responsibility of writing well directly on the employee. That responsibility demands creativity, fresh thinking, care, and study. The employee becomes accountable for personal growth—and mistakes.

2. It enables the employee to own the writing. Research asserts that having a sense of authorship is essential for anyone—adult or child—to want to write and to get better at it. In the corporate world, paper symbolizes not only power but pride. Letting employees sign what they write gives them recognition and credit.

3. It guarantees that better copy is handed in the first time. Giving credit to employees who write well will encourage employees to express themselves the best way they can. Since their signature will now appear, all weaknesses in the correspondence will be attributed to them.

4. It limits the manager's urge to edit the draft to get it to "sound like me." Managers need to know the difference between editing for a reason and editing just to say it the way they would. The compulsion to do the latter

originates from several sources: fear of being blamed themselves for errors; insecurity about how they will be viewed; inability to delegate; need to validate themselves through finding fault in others; acting out their subconscious desire to be a writer.

This is not saying that editing is bad. But when a manager changes "asks" to "requests" and then begins a forty-five-minute debate on which word is better, time is wasted and employee ego battered. Equally disabling to the employee is the manager who makes the change but offers no explanation.

While ghostwriters are paid to adopt the boss's style, better writing is encouraged through practice, acquired through time, and promoted through seminars grounded in the research in writing. Managers who create a hierarchy for editing, focusing on major problems, one at a time, rather than correcting for everything, preserve the integrity of the employee. Such managers tacitly understand what stands out indisputably in the research—that marking every error does little to improve writing ability and may, in fact, do more harm than good.

5. It reveals to the company who really can or cannot write. Managers eager to find ways to improve the quality of writing produced in their department may spend significant time rewriting what their employees have written. But managers who "fix" the writing time after time disable their employees from ever owning what they write, or earning credit—or criticism—for it, and, ultimately, from significantly improving it.

Motivating employees, not merely evaluating them, is part of the managerial role. Creating an endorsement line on business reports and correspondence contributes to this effort. While a write-for-my-endorsement line is not the panacea for poor writing, it is a step forward. After all, isn't growth, rather than perfection, the real goal?

16
Dictating

CAN I CONVINCE YOU TO TRY IT?

*True ease in writing comes from . . . (skill), not chance, as those
move easiest who have learn'd to dance.*

Alexander Pope

While some of us may prefer to compose our business correspondence in longhand or on our Palm Pilots, others may choose the keyboard. Soon, with the quality of speech recognition programs improving daily, "talking our writing"—dictating—directly onto the computer screen may become preferable to our keyboarding it on. For those in fields such as law and medicine, dictating has long been a popular (and often necessary) method of composing correspondence and reports. For them, it has proven itself to be an efficient—and natural—way to keep up with demanding workloads.

Many of us may easily master the mechanics of electronic systems for dictating: which buttons to press when and which keys to code. But we also have to learn how to adapt to a process (dictating) that requires us to "talk writing." Why? What's so difficult about dictating? After all, isn't it just a combination of the habits of speech and the conventions of writing? Well, yes. And no.

While dictating does integrate both worlds, all too often it merges the worst rather than the best of both: the rambling, disorganized flow we find in much speech combined with the stuffiness and triteness we find in much writing—rather than the genuineness and aliveness of effective talking combined with the careful thought and tight organization of effective writing.

Further, it seems that while we've learned to talk naturally, dictating—though it involves speaking—is an acquired skill. It takes more than pressing buttons or opening the mouth to make it work right. It takes sound strategies to integrate the best speaking and writing habits.

The benefits of dictating are worth considering. Machine dictating or using a voice recognition program

- saves time (for dictator and transcriber)
- saves money
- contains more active verbs
- has a simpler vocabulary
- helps communication sound more natural, be more readable
- increases productivity (for you, your office, and your company)
- develops flexibility (machine or computer installed with software is ready when you are)
- develops speaking ability that can help you leave concise phone messages as well.

A PROCESS FOR PRODUCTIVE DICTATING

You've read about the benefits of dictating. Here's how to achieve them.

PHASE ONE: PURPOSEFUL PLANNING

Most successful dictators spend two thirds of their dictating time planning. In fact, for them planning is a necessity, not an option. They plan their general content and order *before* they dictate. They use key words to jog their memory. They plan specific words, phrases, sentences, *while* they dictate. It's not uncommon for dictators to pause every four to eight seconds as they are dictating— to plan the specific words and phrases that will constitute their next sentence or two.

No, they *don't* write out their entire memo, then read it into their micro recorder. Instead, they, as you can, follow a process similar to the one outlined here.

1. Visualize your intended audience(s). Anticipate several audiences.

2. Determine your purpose. This will help you decide on content and organization.

3. Gather information and generate ideas.

4. Generate a simple key-word outline.
   - Eliminate unnecessary parts.
   - Make sure the sequence works.

5. Select and organize your information by numbering it in the sequence in which you want to dictate it.

6. Think about format and how you want to sound.

7. If using a machine, know your equipment. If using a software program, practice with it.

Use a Form Like This to Help You Plan

Productive-Dictation Plan

☐ CONFIDENTIAL

Document Type   ☑ MEMO ☐ LETTER ☐ REPORT ☐ PROPOSAL ☐ OTHER ____

Delivery Method   ☑ E-mail ☐ FAX ☐ MAIL ☐ OVERNIGHT ☐ COURIER

Subject Line   Regaining Mkt Share _____
       TITLE OF REPORT OR PROPOSAL

Audience   To: Field Sales Managers - Region 22
     Copies: Customer Service Manager, Cust. Product Mgr.

Other:

Dictation Options/   ☑ DRAFT   ☑ SPECIAL SPACING 3X spacing

Formal Instructions   ☐ FIRST AND FINAL DRAFT   ☑ ATTACHMENT 12 Mo. Reg 22 Rept.

     ☐ _____   ☐ DATE NEEDED BY _____
      (OTHER)

Purpose   Problem, issue, or concern: Loss of Mkt. Share, R 22 &
     possible causes

     Reference or response to previous communications:
     Region 22 sales comparison, attached

Goal   Focus P/D sales personnel on the problem & get
     corrective action started quickly

Tone   Supportive of field sales personnel but not of results
     Motivational

GENERATE CONTENT, INFORMATION, IDEAS; THEN ELIMINATE UNNECESSARY INFO	ORDER	GENERATE KEY WORD OUTLINE; THEN ARRANGE IN ORDER
We've been losing share in R22 — Impossible to determine why from sls reports	1	Losing share - R22
Only deduction is Mo. stats... & too late	3	Sls reports - count on incr. competition - only mo. results
R22 only region where problem is appearing	2	Problem not in other Rs
Need to pay ++ attention to basics — rte plng. max @ sales call, etc.	6	Product doesn't sell itself - Back to basics
Best product - but doesn't sell itself!	5	Problem doesn't seem to be price or tech. Ask are we covering mkt ?
Need ++ intelligence gathering in mktplace - importance of sls reports	4	More mkt. intell. needed - stress sls reports

Productive-Dictation Plan

☐ CONFIDENTIAL

Document Type   ☐ MEMO ☐ LETTER ☐ REPORT ☐ PROPOSAL ☐ OTHER _____

Delivery Method   ☐ E-mail ☐ FAX ☐ MAIL ☐ OVERNIGHT ☐ COURIER

Subject Line   _____   _____

TITLE OF REPORT OR PROPOSAL

Audience   To:

Copies:

Other:

Dictation Options/   ☐ DRAFT   ☐ SPECIAL SPACING _____

Formal Instructions   ☐ FIRST AND FINAL DRAFT   ☐ ATTACHMENT_____

☐ _____   ☐ DATE NEEDED BY _____

(OTHER)

Purpose   Problem, issue, or concern:

Reference or response to previous communications:

Goal

Tone

GENERATE CONTENT, INFORMATION, IDEAS; THEN ELIMINATE UNNECESSARY INFO	GENERATE KEY WORD OUTLINE; THEN ARRANGE IN ORDER
	ORDER

PHASE TWO: DELIBERATED DICTATING

1. Imagine you are speaking to a person—not a machine.

2. Visualize your final written product so you can give directions to your transcriber (even if it's you) about

    - format
    - spelling
    - punctuation

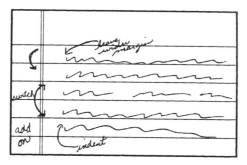

(Unlike the writer, who can draw arrows or add comments in the margin, you must give strictly oral information.)

3. Do on-the-spot planning to

- remember
- select
- avoid repetition
- eliminate rambling, "tacked-on," or awkward phrases typical when we speak.

4. Listen to/review dictation during it. Check for

- precise wording
- redundancies
- rambling, "tacked-on," or awkward phrases.

5. Practice voice control.
   - Use appropriate inflection and pauses.
   - Enunciate clearly. This is the biggest snag for those of you using voice recognition programs.
6. Thank your transcriber.

PHASE THREE: RUTHLESS REVIEWING

1. Listen to your tape for errors if you have used a recorder to dictate and will not have a chance to get your hard copy back to revise; check for
   - redundancies
   - awkward phrases
   - quality of tape/voice.

2. Read your hard copy carefully. Edit for content and tone. And check correctness:
   - nonparallel structure
   - unclear pronoun references
   - inappropriate tense switches
   - wordiness
   - repetition
   - expressions more appropriate to speaking than to writing
   - spelling
   - format
   - punctuation errors.

3. Collaborate with others for suggestions on how to improve.

Appendix:
Guidelines and Model Letters

Customer Follow-up/Recap/Thank you

Confirming/Directive Memos

Encouraging the Team/Team Update

Meeting Minutes

Proposals/Recommendations

Providing/Requesting Information

CUSTOMER FOLLOW-UP / RECAP / THANK YOU

GUIDELINES

1. State right away that your memo is a follow-up, recap, or thank you.

2. Restate all important facts or details that you need to verify or that have changed.

3. Include all relevant details so your reader doesn't need to retrieve information or material supplied earlier.

4. Set a date or way for your reader to contact you if there's a question or need.

5. If it's needed, ask for confirmation. Provide a signature line for your reader if you wish the letter to be a binding contract.

6. Sound genuine. Avoid patronizing your readers or using stale, overused corporatese. Your tone matters.

7. Be specific about what you are thanking your readers for.

8. Restate important facts or details that you need to verify or that have changed.

9. End strong. You can do this by including precise next steps, if any, and a strong positive statement.

10. Consider hand-writing a note rather than sending a formal letter in these situations:

    - when a timely note will be more valued than a formally typed one;
    - when informality and sincerity is accepted and expected; or
    - when being personal will lend credibility.

Customer Follow-up / Recap / Thank You

20 June

Roger Shaw
A&B Distributing
6789 Alpha St.
Ann Arbor, MI 40213

Roger:

We understand—and share—your desire to grow your business during the remainder of this year. To help do so, I have attached the two proposals you asked us to revise when you, Tom Kish, and I met on 16 June.

Getting Promotional Dollars to Pay Dividends	In the proposals we've addressed your concern that although promotional dollars paid directly to Stride Rite Drug from High Energy Corporation are up compared to last year, they are lower than our competition's.
	The revised proposal for a Back to School promotion for August offers a $1.50 per box billback that will be passed on to your retail customers and an additional lump sum advertising allowance.
	The second proposal invites you to include High Energy's King Size Bars in your flyer during October.
Mutual Growth Enjoyed	At our meeting, information provided by both our companies confirmed that High Energy's business with Stride Rite is up and growing at a faster pace than our competition's. This growth is a result of

- increased accessibility at retail and promotional activities for you and your retail customers, and
- merchandising programs, our national advertising campaigns, as well as Stride Rite's efforts.

Together, let's continue to grow. During our next meeting on 10 July, we can discuss these proposals and your plans.

Thank you.

Regards,

Anita Marks

Anita Marks

Customer Follow-up / Recap / Thank You

15 September

Bee Real
Real Good Marketing
7241 Stewart St.
Venice, CA 90292

Dear Bee:

To continue the partnership we've enjoyed this year, I've enclosed the material you requested.

- A quote on your software covers. (Note that our film lamination is less expensive than the U.V. coat.)
- An updated freight cost estimate chart. (I ran the 10 pt cover quantities up to 15,000 and added Maple-Vail to the list.)
- Additional copies for Ernestine, Judy, and Betty.

After you have reviewed this material to assure yourself that we are price competitive, please let me know if you would like us to make any other improvements. You can reach me at (800) 760-0010.

Meanwhile thank you for spending time with me last week and offering feedback on our performance. I look forward to our discussions about next year.

Sincerely,

Tom

Tom Rohlfing, President
Pinnacle Press

Customer Follow-up / Recap / Thank You

FROM:	
To:	
CC:	
BCC:	
SUBJECT:	Thanks for Your Energy

Dear Lynne:

Thank you for your efforts to ensure a successful National Sales Meeting. Your vigor and commitment showed in how smoothly and tastefully all the details of the meeting fit together.

The result of your hard work was a re-energized and focused group—one that assured us of accomplishing our goals to

- roll out our new product line on time,
- follow through our 4Q promotions, and
- exceed our sales numbers!

Again, thank you for your spirit and enthusiastic teamwork. I'm looking forward to your continued energy around the business!

Customer Follow-up / Recap / Thank You

Steve —

Your successes keep multiplying! Good job on being named Region 5 Sales Rep of the month! You've truly dominated your territory.

Congratulations. We're grateful you're on "our side"!

Henry Thorough
Region VP

CONFIRMING / DIRECTIVE MEMOS

GUIDELINES

1. Provide specific instructions and clear directions to be followed. (Be specific without overloading.)

2. Arrange them in an easy-to-retrieve format.

3. If appropriate, express confidence in/thanks for their recent efforts.

4. Stay upbeat.

Confirming / Directive Memos

Date:	2 November
To:	Seymour Sales
From:	Region Manager
Market:	Cleveland
Subject:	**Workwith Confirmation**
Workwith Details:	Date: 5–6 December Place: Distributorship Time: 8:30 A.M.

Objectives: Observe/discuss product market expectations in Cleveland.

1. Identify the critical coverage area
2. Discuss last minute needs
3. Conduct store checks
4. Confirm accuracy of routes

Please Bring:

- Any questions concerning routes and missing stores
- A map showing what your team covers in the market
- An understanding of how closely your routes match retail reality
- Wish list of tools and information needed

Thanks for your efforts.

Confirming / Directive Memos

FROM:	
TO:	
CC:	
BCC:	
SUBJECT:	Business Development Meetings Unscheduled!

Gang,

Just a quick note to notify you that I am unscheduling the Business Development meeting for this week and next. Lots of conflicts, travel and business deadlines for everyone, and I can at least offer this slight relief. However, our weekly Thursday schedule will be in place after this hiatus. (We won't meet on Thanksgiving Day!)

In the meantime, keep the cards and e-mails coming on any critical issues. My door remains open at (almost) all times.

Thanks.

ENCOURAGING THE TEAM

GUIDELINES

1. Generate enthusiasm about new products, POS, services, incentives that they may need to call to their accounts' attention.

2. Supply incentives—concrete and implied, if appropriate.

3. Provide specific instructions and procedures to be followed.

4. And arrange them in an easy-to-retrieve format.

5. Express confidence in their continued success and praise recent contributions.

6. Stay upbeat and informal. Sound sincere rather than superficial. You can do so by avoiding the typical "cheerleading" clichés or by using them cleverly.

Encouraging the Team

FROM:	
TO:	
CC:	
BCC:	
SUBJECT:	Reminder About Phone Forwarding

Hi, Gang!

Yes, this is just a pesky li'l nag-mail: When you are going to be away from your desk for an extended period—and, when you leave for the night—remember to forward your phones to the "DNB" button.

That way, outside callers get connected to your voice mail immediately without having to sit through several rings, only to find you're not there.

Sound picky? Perhaps. But we do get complaints from clients who have to wait, or are rerouted. Thanks for pressing the "DNB" button, rather than our clients' hot button.

Encouraging the Team

FROM:	
To:	
CC:	
BCC:	
SUBJECT:	Teamwork Gets Job Done!

Thanks to both of you for the effort and results you achieved working together this past week calling on Davidson's Markets. The numbers speak for themselves.

- Reset seven Davidson's Markets, gained 43 new items, and discontinued 12 competitive items in the process.

- Sold a counter rack for the top of the soda machine at the checkout and one for the deli counter in the Wilbraham, MA store.

- Sold a lane blocker exclusively for our brands in the Longmeadow, MA store.

What an "above and beyond" performance! Our presence is ever growing—thanks to spirited, enthusiastic teamwork such as yours. I'm looking forward to your continued energy and enthusiasm.

Encouraging the Team

TO: **DATE:**

FROM: **COPIES:**

SUBJECT: A New Year's Wish

Thank you for the spectacular year our office has enjoyed. Our accomplishments have included

- Growth of more than 38%—our best year ever!

- The addition of dozens of new staff members who have brought us new skills, new thinking and top-notch creativity.

- Success across all our account divisions, each of which has built its business, staff and skills over the past 12 months.

- Growth in three distinct ways: 1) an increasing number of accounts that are shared across divisions, 2) new international accounts giving us worldwide responsibility for their products, 3) shared accounts with our other offices and partners.

- Great stability within our senior management team.

- Being named the #1 office in the country.

Of course, not all the news was good, and if I have one wish for the past year it would be that we were able to find the skilled people we needed for our new business faster and with less strain on our existing staff.

I have also heard, rightly I suspect, that in our rush forward, we sometimes didn't do enough to appreciate all the good people in our office and the great work they have done. I pledge to you not to repeat this failing next year.

Again, thank you for all your contributions this year. The contribution each and every one of you makes is important to the whole of our success.

Since I have no doubt that our office will continue to grow and prosper in the new year, I'll focus my New Year's wish on something even more important—a wish for you and your family to enjoy health, happiness and prosperity. Peace be with you.

MEETING MINUTES

GUIDELINES

1. Recap/format meeting discussion and decisions by topic so they're easy to scan.

2. Include status of topic and who is responsible for next steps.

3. Strive for a positive, engaging tone and format. Meeting minutes need not be dull!

4. Include next meeting date information.

Meeting Minutes

TO:
FROM:
SUBJECT: Communication _____Meeting Minutes

14 March _____Meeting Date

ATTENDEES:
DATE: 15 March

Topic	Action	Comments	Status/ Next Step	Respon- sibility
Updating Account Responsibility List	1. Filled out list. 2. Provided code numbers for all accounts.	Includes all new items.	E-mail code sheet shells for updates.	BC
Communication for Retail Stores	♦ Agreed on format & forms to use. ♦ Forward forms to John. ♦ John & Eric will forward info to merchandisers.	Use as calendar planner for entire year.	Jim developing shell & will e-mail copy to you.	JD
Incentive Program	3. Agreed that accounts will supply pricing information.		Reps will supply list of accounts accepting/not accepting program & follow up with surveys.	ED Reps
Display Contest	Steve Davis introduced idea.	♦ May or June. ♦ Run through distributors. ♦ Needs 8-wk. minimum lead time.	Steve, Larry, Monica will look into.	SD LF MS
Next Meeting		In the West Conference Room. See you there!	15 April	

Meeting Minutes

TO:

FROM:

SUBJECT: Communications _____ Meeting Minutes

29 June _____ Meeting Date

ATTENDEES:

DATE: 1 July

Topic	Action	Comments	Status/ Next Step	Respon- sibility
Making Life Easier for Merchandiser, Account Managers, You, & Me	• Agreed on written & oral communication standards. • Agreed that credit policy must have customer's & your signature.	• Will help merchandisers explain & execute credit procedure.	✔	
Monthly Calendar of Retail Events for Merchandisers	• Gives retailers snapshot of priorities by account. • Will elicit promo details from your info sheets.	• Will compile by 3rd week of every month so retailers receive before start of new month.	July calendar attached	WBD
Merchandiser Distribution List on the Way	• Each of you requested a copy.	• You asked for it; you got it! Good idea!	In the mail!	
Store Lists	• Agreed you would provide store lists as needed.	• E-mail me of store openings & closings.	Update as needed	Yours
The Envelope, Please	• Gave each of you envelope with an update of each of your accounts.		Review list to verify info is current. If any info has been highlighted, send requested info to region office by 7/22.	Yours
Next Meeting			8/3	

Many thanks for your participation—and input. Your suggestions have already begun to pay off.

Meeting Minutes

TO:
FROM:
SUBJECT: _____Meeting Minutes

_____Meeting Date

ATTENDEES:
DATE:

Topic	Action	Comments	Status/ Next Step	Respon- sibility

PROPOSALS AND RECOMMENDATIONS

Guidelines

1. State your recommendation or request up front.

2. Be certain that your recommendation considers a need or priority your audience has.

3. State what will be gained from your proposal or request (the benefits!).

4. Provide background information that will help your reader approve your request.

5. Also provide suggestions/alternatives so your reader sees you've thought it out and are flexible. If no alternatives exist, say so.

6. Ask for a response, and give a deadline.

Proposals and Recommendations

TO: **DATE:**

FROM: **COPIES:**

SUBJECT: How to Improve Branded Vending
                    Machine Placement and Profitability

By reviewing—and revamping—our process for placing branded vending machines, we can ensure a more profitable placement of them on Interstate 95. Here is my proposal for accomplishing this.

Require Service Provider to Train Appropriate Personnel in the Mechanics of the Machine

Adequate on-site training for site and vending managers will minimize downtime and errors in stocking, setting prices, movement reporting, etc., which we've experienced in the past.

- If training is unavailable at time of delivery, service provider can return to provide it at a later, agreed upon date.

- When providers merely deliver machines, as has been the case in several instances, the placements fall short of their potential.

Write a More Specific and Shorter Contract

- Stating a specific time frame and payback for exclusive placement ought to give reps leverage. As an example, a $3,500 investment for two years should return the necessary payback.

- Shortening the current seven-page contract will make everyone happier! In fact, we could speed up the administrative process necessary for placement by reducing the contract to one page. The site verification form could appear on one side and the contract on the other.

Consolidate the Best Sales Tools

Why not put together a Branded Vending folder to help pitch these machines? Include

- Machine picture and description
- Contract and Site Verification Form (one-pager)
- Reporting Forms and Movement Retrieval Guide
- Test results—success stores—from other locations

I've enclosed a sample packet for your review.

Proposals and Recommendations

- 2 -

Answer Key Questions to Open the Door Wider to Vending Machine Profitability

1. What contractual timeline will ensure that the Company recoups its investment? Three years? Five years?

2. What is the *time* incrementality of placing branded vending machines? What additional movement can a location expect?

3. Can we include other Branded Vending Success Stories in our selling tools?

4. Under what guidelines should we terminate unprofitable placements?

I'd be willing to be part of the team leading the effort to improve the placements of our branded vending machines.

Let me know when it will be convenient for us to review these recommendations. I'll be available the week of 2 June.

Thanks.

Proposals and Recommendations

TO: **DATE:**

FROM: **COPIES:**

SUBJECT: You Can Make a Difference:
Please Get Ready for Annual United Way Drive

The Company has always had a proud tradition of supporting the United Way, a tireless organization that helps us extend a helping hand to the needy in our communities. And while philanthropy is a personal decision, this year's United Way Drive offers you an opportunity to contribute to an array of charities—or to designate a donation to a specific charity of your choice.

Since my father died last year from Alzheimer's, I have vowed to donate to that cause. I urge you to join me in contributing to a cause that you care about. You can do so with a check or through payroll deductions. The details will follow the first week in September.

Together we can improve the quality of life for everyone. Your part will make a difference.

PROVIDING / REQUESTING INFORMATION

GUIDELINES

1. Tell your reader what you are providing/requesting.

2. If a request, provide the necessary documentation to back it up—and format that information so it is easy for your reader to retrieve.

3. Explain how/why the current situation happened—and, again, steps needed to be taken—and when.

4. Write in a tone that makes your reader want to help or do as you ask.

5. Be appreciative. Thank your reader for prompt service. Invite further inquiries, if appropriate.

Proposals and Recommendations

TO: **DATE:**

FROM: **COPIES:**

SUBJECT: Your Prayers Have Been Answered:
New Plain Paper Fax Machines

Your fax machine woes are over. We have approval to purchase new plain paper fax machines to replace your older ones. The new machine is the Canon Laser Class 5700 plain paper fax, and shipping will begin the week of 2 June.

Here's what you'll need to do:

1. Arrange for someone to be at home to accept delivery. UPS will only stop three times before returning the machine to Staples. You can leave a note for delivery to a neighbor, if necessary.

2. Within 30 days of receiving your new machine, ship back your old one so it may be donated to charity. Please insure it for $200.00 and send it to me at

    > ABC International
    > 3040 Grand Bay Blvd.
    > Tampa, FL 34228

4. If you do not receive a new machine within two weeks of this memo, contact me at 1-800-885-1878 ext. 445.

5. Read the enclosed set up instructions and keep them handy.

Proposals and Recommendations

TO: **DATE:**

FROM: **COPIES:**

SUBJECT: **Your Eyes Needed to Edit National Relaunch Implementation Manual for Chug-a-Lug**

We need your help to ensure we publish one hundred percent correct and up-to-date information on every detail of this program. Toward this goal, we need you to

- thoroughly review the attached draft of the IM.

- clearly write your corrections, additions, deletions, etc. on your copy. Whenever your name is mentioned (in my handwritten notes) you'll need to track down essential information (premium info, forms, original visuals, etc.).

- have your edited version hand delivered to me by Tuesday, September 20 at noon. (You can always give it to me at our status meeting on Tuesday morning . . . Hint! Hint!)

Thanks for your time and feedback. Your full participation is the key to meeting the September 30 deadline about ready to overrun us!

As always, please call me if you have questions (x2019).

Epilogue

Whether you've thumbed casually through the book or labored long and steadfastly from the first to the last chapter, you've been privy to useful and compelling suggestions to help make your workplace writing stand out. My goal has been to show you that your business writing can—and must—be professional, yet personable; sophisticated, yet simple; creative, yet correct.

My hope is that you'll approach future memos and reports with renewed spirit and skill, willing to work on improving one aspect of your writing at a time—whether that is getting started without procrastination or fear; organizing your words with visual and logical appeal; or editing them for clarity, conciseness, correctness, and tone. Don't dilute your efforts by trying to fix all the parts you struggle with simultaneously. Start with the part of the writing process you want to improve most.

If getting started is your roadblock, give yourself permission to say it the wrong way before you say it the right way. Most writing *is* bad before it's good. Avoid fussing over structure and grammar in the early stages. Test your draft on trusted colleagues, to see how an audience reacts to it. Then revise and edit based on feedback and suggestions, and your own rethinking.

This book ends with a key item for your workplace writing survival kit: a Writer's Checklist. Use it *before* sending out your memos, letters, and reports. It will faithfully remind you what works, what won't.

When I began writing the first edition of this book, my son, Eric, teasingly said, "Mom, you know more about writing than people really want to know." I'm betting he's wrong.

Good luck and good writing.

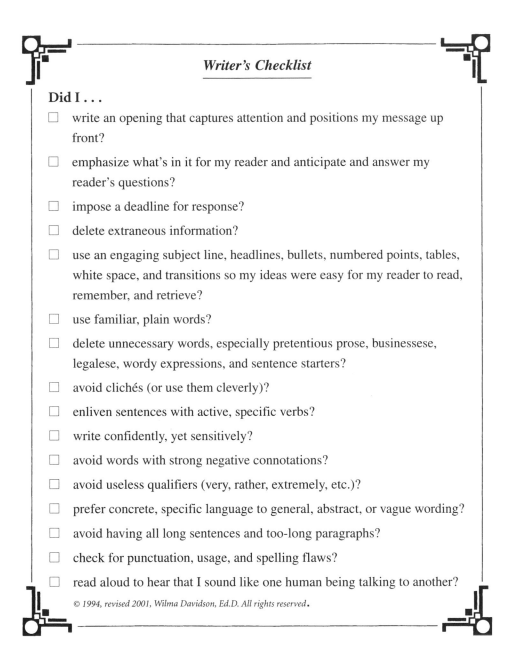

Writer's Checklist

Did I . . .

- ☐ write an opening that captures attention and positions my message up front?

- ☐ emphasize what's in it for my reader and anticipate and answer my reader's questions?

- ☐ impose a deadline for response?

- ☐ delete extraneous information?

- ☐ use an engaging subject line, headlines, bullets, numbered points, tables, white space, and transitions so my ideas were easy for my reader to read, remember, and retrieve?

- ☐ use familiar, plain words?

- ☐ delete unnecessary words, especially pretentious prose, businessese, legalese, wordy expressions, and sentence starters?

- ☐ avoid clichés (or use them cleverly)?

- ☐ enliven sentences with active, specific verbs?

- ☐ write confidently, yet sensitively?

- ☐ avoid words with strong negative connotations?

- ☐ avoid useless qualifiers (very, rather, extremely, etc.)?

- ☐ prefer concrete, specific language to general, abstract, or vague wording?

- ☐ avoid having all long sentences and too-long paragraphs?

- ☐ check for punctuation, usage, and spelling flaws?

- ☐ read aloud to hear that I sound like one human being talking to another?

Bibliography

Davidson, Wilma. *Managing Your Writing*. Self-published, 1982.

———. "Write Department" columns. *Raritan Valley Business Review*, August 1987, p. 12. January, February, March, 1988.

Davidson, Wilma, and Booher, E. Kathleen. *The Davidson and Booher Training Manual*. Self-published, 1980.

———. "Eleven Myths About Writing." *Training*, April 1982, pp. 40–42.

Elbow, Peter. *Writing with Power*. New York: Oxford University Press, 1981.

Flesch, R. *How to Write Plain English*. New York: Barnes & Noble, 1979.

Gordon, Karen Elizabeth. *The Transitive Vampire: A Handbook of Grammar for the Innocent, the Eager, and the Doomed*. New York: Times Books, 1984.

———. *The Well-Tempered Sentence: A Punctuation Handbook for the Innocent, the Eager, and the Doomed*. New York: Ticknor & Fields, 1983.

Gunning, R. *The Technique of Clear Writing*. New York: McGraw-Hill, 1952.

Howard, V. A., and Barton, J. H. *Thinking on Paper*. New York: William Morrow and Co., 1986.

Ivers, Mitchell. *The Random House Guide to Good Writing*. New York: Random House, 1991.

Kane, Thomas S. *The New Oxford Guide to Writing*. New York: Oxford University Press, 1988.

Maggio, Rosalie. *The Dictionary of Bias-Free Usage*. Phoenix: Oryx Press, 1991.

Rico, Gabrielle Lusser. *Writing the Natural Way*. Boston: Houghton-Mifflin, 1983.

Stevens, K. T., Stevens, K. C., and Stevens, W. P. "Measuring the Readability of Business Writing." *The Journal of Business Communication* 29 (1992): 367–382.

Strunk, William, and White, E. B. *The Elements of Style*. 4th ed. New York: Macmillan, 1999.

Venolia, Jan. *Rewrite Right!* Berkeley, Calif.: Ten Speed Press/Periwinkle Press, 2000.

———. *Write Right!* Berkeley, Calif.: Ten Speed Press/Periwinkle Press, 1995.

Zinsser, William. *On Writing Well*. New York: Harper & Row, 1998

Index